THE SUPERNATURAL: THE PLACE I MEET GOD

RENA WILBURN

authorHOUSE®

AuthorHouse™
1663 Liberty Drive
Bloomington, IN 47403
www.authorhouse.com
Phone: 833-262-8899

Published by AuthorHouse 04/30/2021

ISBN: 978-1-6655-2185-7 (sc)
ISBN: 978-1-6655-2186-4 (e)

Library of Congress Control Number: 2021907229

Print information available on the last page.

This book is printed on acid-free paper.

Scripture quotations marked KJV are from the Holy Bible, King James Version
(Authorized Version). First published in 1611. Quoted from the KJV Classic
Reference Bible, Copyright © 1983 by The Zondervan Corporation.

CONTENTS

REFERENCE: SCRIPTURES

PREFACE

I dedicate this book in loving memories to all the special people who God has bought in my life to teach, guide, and make me into the person I am today. I'd especially like to thank my parents, Willie and Julia Carter, whose love and life taught me by word and example everything great parents teach their children. Most importantly, they introduced me to a God who loves me and whose love even surpassed their own.

Love you, Mom and Dad.

I thank God for the people currently in my life who have been such a blessing to help and encourage me along the way. The saying "No Man is an Island" I found to be true. No one really succeeds on their own without God. However, we need one another. We are here on this planet only but for a short period of time, a moment in comparison to eternity, but the impact of our lives on others can last many moments throughout generations. My prayer is that this book will locate you in some aspect, help, comfort, and encourage you as you walk through your journey… Your journey call Life…

I'd like to give special thanks to my sister Nancy Jones for all her help and support. Most importantly her believing that with God's help, I could write this book. Thank you for your insight and creativity to bring this assignment from God to a successful end. I owe you one.

Blessings… Rea

FOREWORD

Donna Harney (Playwright – Vision on High Productions – Homeless But Hopeful Organizer) - *The book THE SUPERNATURAL THE PLACE I MEET GOD... is attentive to the Spirit of God. It is powerful prophetic ammunition of inspiration, interpretation, and divine revelation communicated by an all-knowing powerful God of wisdom. It helps you to experience and desire a richer walk with God.*

Gloria Womack (Founder - Call Unto Me Ministry) - *Your story (Johnathan's Story) demonstrated the power of prayer and the faith to believe. When you call, He will answer.*

Bishop Peter Fenton (Pastor - First Samuel (W)Holistic Ministry) - *We offer congratulations and blessings to the author of this book. This book, The Supernatural The Place I Meet God is biblically sound, empowering, and rich with the workmanship of Elohim's (God's) Scriptures. The author of this book challenges each reader to review his or her spiritual location-position; therefore, to the author, an awesome job.*

Pastor (Elder) Calvin Gordon (Call Unto Me Ministry – ChurchTalk Radio Coordinator) - *I was truly blessed to be able to read this chapter on the power and Death and Life (Jonathan's Story). "Faith grows as we exercise it." What a powerful opening statement. As I read Chapter one, I was totally captivated right from the very beginning to the end. As I continued reading with anticipation, I could feel the power of God's presence. The story reminded me of the many miracles that I've witnessed in my life. The writer Prophetess Wilburn (Rena) took the time to back up the story with scripture which I felt was so important and helpful. I particularly appreciated her honesty about her own faith. I'm looking forward to reading this book in its entirety.*

Co-Pastor Florida Lawrence (Shining Star Missionary Baptist Church) - *Great, Great Book!!! The flow was excellent. The stories were anointed and filled with explosive expectations of the moves of God. I will definitely recommend this book to be used as a teaching tool for churches, congregations, and individuals; I know I will.*

Nancy Jones (Sister) - *The SuperNatural: The place I meet God. How fitting a title for this is what our world truly needs. God continues to remind us through his Words, deeds, actions, dreams, miracles, and power that He is here. With God, all things are possible. His super and our natural combined to create limitless possibilities from a SuperNatural God, intervening on our behalf for the things we individually or corporately need and even desire.*

INTRODUCTION

The Supernatural is defined by Merriam-Webster as: of or relating to an order of existence beyond the visible observable universe; especially: of or relating to God or a god, demigod, spirit, or devil.

Truly life is a journey. There are so many ups and downs. Tragedies and Testimonies. The seen and unseen world of the supernatural is amazing. Many people only look at surface happenings but fail to realize and embrace the unseen world: The SuperNatural. Whether or not it is believed, there is a supernatural realm that is definitely involved in our destiny's outcome effects. In my life's journey, I've encountered the world of the Supernatural, both good and evil. Meeting with the Creator of the Universe can be a mind-blowing experience. How awesome it must have been for Adam to meet with God on a daily basis; then the devastation and chaos of that relationship being severed because of his disobedience. However, we have been given another chance to tap into the supernatural realm of the spirit.

The SuperNatural is the place I meet God and most importantly where He meets me. It is a place where my natural is transformed by His supernatural— limitless, endless possibilities await me. A place where miracles, signs, and wonders happen. Where He embraces me and the warmth of His love and the awesomeness of His power make me believe that all things are possible. Finally, it's a place where time and space are suspended, and we step into eternity.

"Come along with me and dare to believe
that you can experience it too."

CHAPTER ONE

THE POWER OF DEATH AND LIFE
(JONATHAN'S STORY)

Scripture:

Isaiah 65:24 - And it shall come to pass, that before they call, I will answer; and while they are yet speaking, I will hear.

Story:

Faith grows as we exercise it. Remembering one summer, as it was custom, my old high school friends would get together and play basketball. This particular year the game was held at the park with a BBQ afterward. It was so much fun. I teased the players about taking Advil and rubbing down with BENGAY because even though they loved the game, some had put on a few pounds, and being a little older, they weren't what they used to be, yet they still had skills. After the game, I saw Adam sitting alone on a bench. I thought he was just getting himself together, and I went over to talk to him. He told me that his legs were cramping so bad.

Thinking that it was because he wasn't as young as he used to be, I laid my hands on his knees, and I left. Suddenly, I see him jumping around. What was going on? At that point, I walked back over to him. He said the pain had stopped. I began to speak to him prophetically about things he hadn't shared with us. He had torn his Achilles, and because of the fear of the pain, he'd stopped playing; therefore, he wasn't in any shape to play the game. Instantly God had stopped the pain, healed him, and taken away the fear. (2 Tim 1:7) Flowing in the healing anointing is awesome.

After the BBQ, we met at Deborah's house and there was Adam, sharing what God had done for him openly and unashamedly. I loved it. He was growing in faith in the fact that God does answer prayer. This incident would prepare him for the story I'm going to share with you now.

Jonathan's Story:

There was nothing unusual about this morning as I sat at my computer ready to address the journey of internet surfing, praying for the sick, and the day-to-day things I do every day religiously. The phone rings, it's Adam. He's somber, almost in tears. I could hear it in his voice. Something was wrong. "Rena, please pray for Jonathan. He's not breathing and they just took him in an ambulance to the hospital. I'm on my way there." Not the words I wanted to hear first thing in the morning. I said, "Okay." Jonathan had a stroke that paralyzed his right side and he's not breathing. Things didn't look good. Now faced with this life and death situation with Jonathan, Adam could start using his faith to believe because he'd experienced answers to prayer before. (2 Thess 1:3-4)

Jonathan was not of our faith. There was a time; I would have struggled with his request, not to pray, but to believe because he was not a considered covenant son. However, I'd recently been taught that it wasn't our goodness or our righteousness that was the basis of answered prayer.

It was because of God's love for us (John 3:16-17) and the covenant (1Peter 2:24) we (covenant sons) have with him in the blood of Jesus that we get answers to prayer (the prayer of faith).

Hanging up the phone, I stopped what I was doing. It was praying time, but something strange happened before I could start my long war fighting prayer. I'd gotten great results with this type of praying through the years, but at the price of total exhaustion. God interrupted the scene with these words, "What do you want me to do?" I hadn't asked, hadn't petitioned. He'd been listening, and he cared and wanted to help. (Isa 65:24, Mat 6:8)

He was not doing things in-line or in the order I'd come to know. Simplicity of prayer, no superfluous of words, he would later tell me (Matt 6:7-8 - But when ye pray, use not vain repetitions, as the heathen do: for they think that they shall be heard for their much speaking). "What do you want me to do?" What a question God had presented to me. It was both caring and comforting. At that point, I knew he would help us; he would answer our prayers. I said, "Heal him; he doesn't know you." (1 John 5:14-15)

I remember the same call years before about my father being rushed to the hospital. It's wasn't a great feeling. He had passed before we got there. For years he'd said that man really only lives for 70 years. He died at 69½. Thank God he was saved. I didn't want to go through this again, at least not at this moment. I asked God to reveal himself to Jonathan supernaturally.

Meanwhile, the family had been called to the hospital: the doctors didn't think he would make it. He'd been stroking out, so time was of the essence. I learned later Adam's son (not yet committed to the Lord) asked was he going to die. Adam said, "No, I called Rena, and she's praying." Adam had faith in my faith. The only problem with that is my faith waiver at times. When my faith is in God, his love, and faithfulness and not my ability (but my availability), then and only then can I rest in the assurance that He will handle everything with or without me. (Mark 11:22, Matt 7:7-8)

Faith placed in anyone outside of God often-times yields very disappointing results. We sometimes make promises but are unable to keep them. Our faith should be ever-increasing as we walk with God. Every trial should strengthen it, not decrease it. However, that's not always an easy task when our emotions are screaming at us, "It's not going to work. It's not going to work this time".

Don't let time fool you. With life as an open book unto the face of God, we travel throughout this lifetime in the ups and downs of its winding corridors, depending on God's grace alone to lead and guide us into paths of victory and righteousness. God stands outside of time, orchestrating our lives bringing about eternal victories. He will never fail us. We are in good hands.

Heb 13:5 … for he hath said, I will never
leave thee, nor forsake thee.

Adam said he felt better after he asked me to pray, just like I always felt when I asked my mom to pray for me. People can carry you on their prayers for just so long, and then one day you'll have to stand alone using your own faith. Faith is not a feeling. If the enemy can hold you in the arena of feeling, he will defeat you, but if you hold him in the arena of faith, it will enforce his already Calvary defeat. Adam said that the doctors told him many things were wrong with Jonathan and they didn't think he was going to make it. (Heb 11:1, Col 2:15)

Because Adam didn't call to give me an update on Jonathan's condition, I reached out to my intercessory prayer friends and asked them to pray. They're some great prayer warriors and always ready to pray at the drop of a hat. (Matt 18:20) After sending them the message to pray, I decided to call him to see what was happening. He said I was thinking about you just before you called. Jeremiah had asked if I'd called you back." Jonathan was now fine and the doctors were keeping him overnight just for observation. And oh, by the way, he now had some use of his right hand, which he didn't have before because of the stroke. Adam should have called earlier, but I forgave him because I'm such a good friend.

What an Awesome God we serve. What a Wonderful Father he is. Truthfully, I'd never expected such a quick answer to prayer. Adam had experienced a real bonafide miracle. From a prognosis of he's stroking out, and we don't think he's going to make it to a prognosis, he's fine and we're going to watch him overnight, which is nothing short of a miracle.

Lessons Learned:

God heals based on his love and our faith in the covenant we have in the blood of Jesus Christ. When we ask based on these two principles along with thanksgiving, we can expect marvelous and magnificent results, even miracles.

We are but natural men, yet we have a supernatural Father, a God that can do anything. Nothing is impossible for him. He had volunteered his help, his strength, and his might before I ever asked, so I took him up on his offer. Adam and Jeremiah had watched the faithfulness of God in action. They'd seen prayer requested and prayer answered. What a testimony? To God be the glory. What a great Father he is! (Isa 65:24)

When we believe by faith that we have the petition of what we desire of him, we must always give "Thanks." Never forget to give thanks. I call it the Power of Prayer and Praise (Phil 4:6).

Prophetic Words:

We will see more answers to prayer when we pray based on God's love and faithfulness and not the faithfulness of the person we're praying for or our faithfulness, for that matter.

Superfluous words won't get the job done either; the only things needed are the knowledge of the Love of God and our Covenant Rights in the Name of Jesus.

What the word says, God will do. Only Believe...

CHAPTER TWO

HOW TO RECEIVE

Scripture:

*Mark 11:24 - Therefore I say unto you, What things soever ye desire, when ye pray, believe **that ye receive them**, and ye shall have them.*

Story:

As I sat in what appeared as the ashes of my life, I wonder what had gone wrong. My heart was broken; I was sick, broke, discouraged, and couldn't figure out how I got here. I knew the scriptures. I'd watched God use my spiritual gifts to help others, even people I'd never met, yet my life was in total chaos. (Ps 34:19)

How can I speak into other people's lives, lay hands on the sick, and see them recover, yet my life is such a mess, those words haunted me? Where did I miss it? Me the prophetic one, desperately needing a word from the Lord. I asked everybody I could think of for a word only to become even more frustrated because their words were all futuristic; I needed a now word and move of God. (Mark 16:17-18, Prov 15:23)

All my life, God had blessed me to be a blessing; however, at that moment, I stood on the edge of bankruptcy. I watched the enemy come in like a flood against my finances, my family, and my friends. I know what it is to become paralyzed by debt. It wasn't that I'd overspent. How could this happen, I was a tither, and I love to give. I was almost afraid to ask someone for help because they would soon come under attack. Only God could get me out of this mess. Pastor Bill Winston said God had to be your source, your only source. Everything else is a resource. If God isn't your source, there is very little hope or stability in your situation. (Isa 59:19)

Remembering the time I'd volunteered at the Red Cross, I received a call that so touched my heart from a Katrina victim who was going through this same thing. I wasn't working at the time, so I'd volunteered to help the Red Cross with this particular crisis. Gas prices were the highest they'd ever been and the Red Cross was not close to where I lived. Talk was cheap; I had to do something to help these people. It would be sowing seeds into their lives. Daughters of Zion and Shining Star MBC took up offerings to sponsor me (buy gas) to volunteer at the Command Station.

The caller was desperate in need of help, yet the center could offer very little as it was inundated with calls at that point. She was a tither; she had lost everything in the storm, had no one to help her and now had no money. Her daughter was very sick and without her medication had become suicidal. I could feel her pain as she spoke every word. Where was God in the midst of all of her troubles? He had spared her life and the life of her daughter, yet she stood in the ashes and ruins of what was once a good life. People are good at giving you scriptures when money would work at that moment. She wasn't looking for scriptures. She needed monetary help. We'd been instructed just to let the people talk, so I did.

Their stories were heart-wrenching. I could feel their sense of loss. I was in the perfect place to help them as I was traveling down that road myself. I could tell the caller was becoming a little bitter. (James 2:15-16)

If I had the money, I would have sent it to her. She was expressing what I'd felt, but I didn't get to say it openly because I'm a minister. The strange thing about this story is that even though she and others like her were facing complete loss, and while some were very sick even terminal, they were the nicest people I'd ever spoken with. Many just needed to hear someone's voice, someone to give them hope and direction. Someone to listen and care about them; today, that would be me. When I told them I was in ministry and would pray for them, they were so appreciative. I knew what it was to suffer pain and loss. It wasn't on the same scale, but lost is lost, and pain is pain. I've learned never to minimize someone's pain, just because it wasn't mine. (2 Cor 1:3-4)

In my situation, sad to say, like the caller, I'd gotten bitter and not better. I'd lost my passion. How could God, my Father, see me suffering and not deliver me? I had been years in the waiting. Every time I tried to get up, I was knocked back down. I never cut off my relationship with God, but it was strained. He told me every day he loved me. If it had not been for that, I think I would have just walked away from ministry and life. "Stats say that 250 people leave ministry every month, 53 percent are often concerned about their family's financial security, 48 percent often feel the demands of ministry are more than they can handle, 21 percent say their church has unrealistic expectation of them, 54 percent find the role of pastor frequently overwhelming, 84 percent say they're on call 24 hours a day" (Dance, 2016). I needed HELP… (1 John 4:16, 1 John 3:1)

God miraculously gave me a job that paid off half my debts and I got my house out of foreclosure (2-year process). I hadn't even applied for the job; someone called and asked if I would be interested in the position. Abruptly the job ended. That's the problem with contract work; it can end without notice. It took six months before my unemployment kicked in. After six months, my unemployment ran out. I prayed, Oh God, please HELP me. I've been here before. Struggling, I continued to do the things I knew to do. However, this time, I'm watching my words and asking God to help me with my words and attitude. Bad things happen to good people, and good things happen to bad people, but God in his infinite wisdom will work it out for your good and his glory, if you let him, if you don't give up, which is the hope for the Child of God. (Rom 8:28)

It was after I saw a post on Facebook that said, "Even when times are bad, God is good," that things began to change for me. It spoke to the depths of my heart and soul. I knew it was time to move on, to begin again. I had been stuck. It felt like I'd gotten off the world while the world kept on turning. I knew I wasn't going to defeat my personal demons without getting it right with God first. The thing about God was He was there all the time. He told me he loved me and I would tell him I loved him, but my heart wasn't in it. I'd become numb. If I had any emotions, they were negative.

People can be so mean and cruel when you owe them or come to them for help. Facing repossession of the second car, the guy from the loan company screaming at me, "If you haven't gotten a job by now, what makes you think you're going to get one." I was devastated. I needed to quiet my soul so that I could find the peace I needed to hear a clear and precise word from the Lord, but this wasn't the day. The public assistance office woman humiliated me as I stood in line for assistance with my utility bill. She was so loud that everybody got quiet as she spoke to me as if I was nothing. Man, did that hurt. I took it because I needed help. The next girl to assist me was so kind and said, I'm going to do everything I can to help you (It still brings tears to my eyes).

Isaiah 61:3 - To appoint unto them that mourn in Zion, to give unto them beauty for ashes, the oil of joy for mourning, the garment of praise for the spirit of heaviness; that they might be called trees of righteousness, the planting of the LORD, that he might be glorified.

It had been years, and I struggled living in poverty, jobless, and many times feeling hopeless. So hopeless that if I hadn't known the scriptures, I would have contemplated suicide. I felt such a sense of loss until you just want to go to sleep and never wake up. People treat you differently when you are poor; they can make you feel like you're less-than. Disrespect and shame grasped my heart. How did I get here? What had I done wrong? When was the restoration that I preached about coming my way? Where was the God that restores? He told me every day that He loved me, but I lived in poverty and shame. Poverty is a curse and Christ has redeemed us from the curse to be blessed. I knew poverty and lack were not the ultimate plan of God for me. (Jer 29:11-13, Gal 3:13-14)

I knew if I was ever going to get out of this mess, I had to continue to praise God, even if I didn't feel like it. I had to find my lost praise, my sacrifice of praise. I learned that faith is not feeling. It can produce feelings, but it was not feeling. Sometimes you just have to go with your faith, and your feelings will eventually follow.

I remember the day I told God I was sorry I was mad at him. It wasn't like he was surprised.

He didn't fall off his throne from shock. He was so forgiving. Something in me instantly changed. I felt a freedom at that moment to really praise again. The strain between us had gone. I knew he hadn't caused people to do evil against me, but I needed restoration and he was my only hope, my only help, my only source.

The bible says in everything give thanks. In everything is not the same as for everything. In every situation, you must believe that God:

1) *Knows everything and is never taken by surprise*
2) *Is good and he loves you*
3) *Will work all things together (good, bad, and indifferent) for your good.*

You in turn must:

1) *Watch your words*
2) *Watch your attitude; it will determine your altitude*
   You will rise only as high as your words
3) *Words are powerful. They make us like God (Father), Like Father, Like Son*
4) *Declare and decree the word of God only*
5) *Command your morning as described in Job 38:12.*

Sitting in my favorite chair, I heard God finally speak into the darkness of my situation, "The problem isn't that I haven't given; it's that you haven't received." When you're in disobedience, you can't get your faith to work, but what's funny, my faith was working fine for everyone else. He wanted me to write this book, but I didn't have a clue how, so I just didn't do it. I couldn't put my mind around the whole thing. What do I have to say that others haven't already said and better? Who would listen to me? What I didn't know was God was going to open up the revelation on receiving, but not until I did the last thing he'd told me. Feeling inadequate isn't an excuse for not doing whatever impossible task God has called you to do because he never intended for you to do it alone. He always factors himself in the equation; that's why so many people fail who try to make it without him. Success = God + Me... (Zech 4:6, Mark 16:20)

At the time, Pastor Bill Winston began teaching on the subject of man being a speaking being. You receive by the words you speak. It was just that simple. It wasn't something that I didn't know, but something that I neglected. I would speak over other people's lives and see miraculous results, but I was ignoring basic biblical truths because I was too emotionally involved in my own problems. Brother Kenneth E. Hagin taught the concept of having what you say, but the pressures of life had crowded it out. I considered Brother Hagin a mentor. I bought many of his books and tapes, listened to his radio and TV programs, and even attended several of his Faith Seminars where he shook my hand as a partner. I wrote to him once and actually received a personal reply that I will always cherish. It's not enough to know what to do. Knowing is only step one in the process; you must speak it and then do it. (Mark 4:19)

Mark 11:23-24 - For verily I say unto you, That whosoever shall say unto this mountain, Be thou removed, and be thou cast into the sea; and shall not doubt (diakritheé – stand condemned)in his heart, but shall believe that those things which he saith shall come to pass; he shall have whatsoever he saith. 24 Therefore I say unto you, What things soever ye desire, when ye pray, believe that ye receive them, and ye shall have them.

I told God my life doesn't look anything like the Word, He said, "Then it's not over." When what we see is not what we want, it's not over until what we see aligns itself with the word/will of God. We can use our words to change that which is seen. God said, "If you can't see it, you'll never begin to say it and change your world." Since the fall of Adam, this world is set up for our defeat and destruction. Everywhere you look, it's death, darkness, and devastation, but we've (those in Christ: the second Adam) been called to dispel the darkness and bring light and life, to bring order out of chaos; victory out of defeat. (2 Cor 4:18, Gen 1:3)

We must renew our minds to the Word of the Living God. Everything starts with your believing, which in-turn will formulate your words, Words of Faith or Words of Fatality. Our words are many times aligned with our problem (we rehearse them to anybody who will listen and that includes speaking them to ourselves). When our words are aligned with the word of God, things happen and they happen more quickly. I love the suddenlies of God. It's not in the abundance of man's words but words given by the inspiration of the Spirit of God, in line with the will of God that bring about change. If people only knew how powerful their words are, they would be careful what they repetitively say/ speak. Faith comes by hearing, but it is activated and received by speaking…

If things are not in line with the word of God, then it's not over. How you see yourself and how you see God has a lot to do with receiving from Him. See yourself in prayer as going to a fountain that is already turned on (not that you have to turn it on by your prayers), then just jump in. See yourself as going through a door that's already opened (not one that closed that you have to beat down to open), then go through. See God as a Good-Father there to lift you up, not one that's just waiting with a hammer to beat you down. (Rom 10:17, Heb 4:12)

Ironically, I remembered a prophetic word God had given me over twenty years before: "I will teach you so that you can teach my people. I'll teach you to teach them how to worship, reverence and receive from me and nothing shall be impossible to those that believe and receive from me, saith the Lord of Host" 2/11/91. I'd never paid much attention to the receiving part, but now it was crucial to getting out of debt, getting healthy, and moving on. God taught me how to receive and write the end of the story of my life with my words.

Sad to say, I went from negative words to no words, which are just as bad. Those times when I didn't say anything, nothing was being established. You have to take off the old, but you have to put on the new.

"W. O. R. D. S"

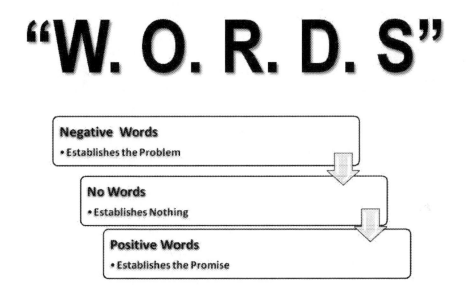

Negative Words
- Establishes the Problem

No Words
- Establishes Nothing

Positive Words
- Establishes the Promise

Your Choice, Your Call...

Watch Negative Words

Satan: 1) Uses your negative words to try to destroy you, 2) He tries to discredit your reputation to silence your voice (your words). We have to be careful of the lives we live as our reputation and character are on the line. People will not receive from you if they don't believe in you (your words). A man is only as good as his word. If you try to protect your reputation rather than your character, you are going to fail. God keeps your reputation while he trains you to keep your character. Satan uses lies to destroy your reputation, even by well-meaning people just passing on what they'd heard. Be careful what you hear because lies are often dressed up in enough truth that makes it totally believable. When a man's reputation is destroyed, people will not accept his teaching, even if it's from God. (Prov 22:1)

I began to speak into my darkness, words of light... If I truly believe what the word of God had revealed, I had first to see things as God sees them, then I had to speak what I saw to evoke change or, as it is said today: Bring order to disorder. It wasn't easy because, by this point, I had become accustomed to seeing and saying things like it was. I knew better. After I surrendered to his will, God sent great messages from different ministers to confirm what he was saying to me. Listening to Joel Osteen was such a blessing in those days. I called him the Minister of Hope long before he received that title by the world. He never painted a picture of a life without struggles but a life of victory through Christ. It was just awesome. (Heb 11:1, Matt 17:20)

2 Cor 4:11 - We having the same spirit of faith, according as it is written, I believed, and therefore have I spoken; we also believe, and therefore speak;

I began to watch my words and began to speak those things that be not as tho they were. My friend and prayer partner, DeAnne Phillips told me, God said to write what you wanted, so I did.

I started to ask for Big Things to see my dreams come true. Blessed and a Blessing. Truly it's more blessed (to have) to give than to receive. Eph 3:20 - Now unto him that is able to do exceeding abundantly above all that we ask or think, according to the power that worketh in us.

Lessons Learned:

You are a speaking being; your words create your world

Speak into the darkness... light... (Light Be)

Don't continue rehearsing your problems; it makes them bigger, and there ain't anything or anybody bigger than your God

If your life or circumstance doesn't align itself with the Word, use your words to bring it into alignment

We've been called to dispel the darkness and bring light and life... to bring order out of chaos, victory out of defeat

When you're in disobedience, your faith is hindered because your heart will condemn you. Repent and Move on (No Condemnation)

We received by faith as we speak the Word of God and believe in his love, his faithfulness, and his covenant of Grace

The comfort God gives us in our trials, he expects us to give to others.

Prophetic Words:

When what we see is not in line with the word of God, it's not over.

If you can't see it, you'll never begin to say it and change your world.

How you receive is to speak it (speak what you want to see, speak what God has already spoken).

The problem isn't that I (God) haven't given; it's that you haven't received (ask God to help you receive).

We receive by the words we speak and by adding Praise and Thanksgiving.

"I will teach you so that you can teach my people. I'll teach you to teach them how to worship, reverence and receive from me and nothing shall be impossible to those that believe and receive from me, saith the Lord of Host" 2/11/91.

Feeling inadequate isn't an excuse for not doing whatever impossible task God has called you to do because he never intended for you to do it alone.

CHAPTER THREE

NEW SEASON OF GRACE

Scripture:

Eccl 3:1 - To everything there is a season, and a time to every purpose under the heaven:

To everything, there is a season, as the writer of Proverbs states so eloquently. The problem is change is not always a welcome entity. However, seasons change, and our lives change with or without our blessings. Many of the changes in my seasons weren't received well and I struggled. Some changes I handled so badly that I got the privilege to take over until I got them right. It's funny now, I can see myself kicking and screaming like a brat, but God was so patient. He had no problem giving me re-tests. This story tells my life's progression from being called to the ministry until walking in the anointing I was called to do and a few major lessons I learned in between.

Story:

From my earliest childhood memories, God was teaching and moving me into the spiritual realm, the realm of the supernatural. Unfortunately, it had to be done outside of the traditional church teaching I was receiving. As I look back today, I see it was in those times I would have to choose who (what spirit) would cultivate the gifting in me. One of my first recollections of the prophetic move of God in my life was as a first-grader. I'd been sent to a second-grade class to get supplies for my teacher. Upon arriving, the teacher was orally quizzing her students. She asked the first science question. The class didn't know the answer. As and I opened my mouth to speak with the assistant about the supplies, unbeknownst to me, I answered the question. The assistant said, "This first grader just answered the question." I didn't hear the question and I didn't hear myself answer it. She asked me to repeat the answer. I opened my mouth again to tell her I didn't hear the question and again I answered it. This time I heard it. Afterward, I thought now that was weird, so I dismissed it. Besides, no one in their right mind would believe me if I told them. Little did I know what God had in store for me in the coming years concerning the prophetic anointing.

(Jer 1:5 - Before I formed thee in the belly I knew thee, and before thou camest forth out of the womb I sanctified thee, and I ordained thee a prophet unto the nations.)

Call to Ministry

What I learned about the spiritual realm with no leadership was hit and miss. Uncharted territory. Trial and Error, mostly error. Every Saturday, I would take a long long soak bath while singing praises to God until I looked like a wrinkled prune. I loved to sing, just like my mom, just not as good. I sang whatever came up out of my spirit, new, old, or made up; it didn't matter. One particular morning in 1982, something happened that surprised even me. As I was transitioning into my next song, I opened my mouth and I heard these words:

"The Spirit of the Lord is upon me, because he hath anointed me to preach the gospel to the poor; he hath sent me to heal the brokenhearted, to preach deliverance to the captives, and recovering of sight to the blind, to set at liberty them that are bruised." (Luke 4:18)

Thinking where did that come from, I kept on singing. Many years later, I discovered it was a scripture and began my search to find why God had interrupted my bath that Saturday morning. It was then; I learned he was calling me to preach the gospel in a traditional church that didn't believe in women preachers. I was told, "You may be called, but no woman will ever preach in my church." God has a sense of humor. I didn't handle it very well, neither did my leadership, but I was determined to pursue my calling, so eventually, in 1989, it was time to leave. (Phil 3:13-14)

I continued studying the scriptures and used my prophetic and teaching gifts at another church and other places where doors were opened to women. Even with studying and learning, there will come a time when God will begin to transition, tweak, and plain-o change and interrupt your theology. Shifting occurs when it's time for new levels, new dimensions, and new challenges to take place in both the natural and spiritual realms. I heard someone say, new levels, new devils. I tend to agree. It was a painful process. I'm not very good with change. I went kicking and screaming.

In 1997, I was ordained as a minister of the gospel by Pastor Lonnie Roundtree. In 2003, we formed a women's outreach called Daughters of Zion. We primarily support other women in ministry as well as our community, reaching beyond denominational lines. Yearly we hold a Women's Conference where we invite different ministries to participate and fellowship. The conferences are always so empowering as the Holy Spirit leads His daughters into praise, worship, and the word. God had a plan and purpose for my life, and now I had an open door to fulfill my calling and help other struggling women do the same.

Prophetic Calling – Assist in the gathering of the Last Harvest

Another phase in my venture was to address the prophetic calling on my life concerning the End-Time Harvest. (Rom 12:2)

I was reading an Item that said, "It is finished," when God spoke, "Rena, the time is short, and I must have people (children) that will both hear and obey my word however it comes. Many are dying or inline, on their way to hell because there aren't enough laborers telling the "Good News" with joy, thus bringing in the mass of End-Time Event Harvest (I believe this is the "Special Work" that the man (angel) told me about years ago. You've been chosen to assist in the gathering of the last Harvest. So don't be discouraged or dismayed – Remember that my time is not your time, and my ways are not your ways (Set Time). But it shall come to past as I have said, just like I said. – Saith the Lord.

I was so excited and thought this is great, but the enemy also heard these words and set out to stop me at every turn. I met opposition from everywhere, even people who said they loved me. Of course, I made mistakes. It's hard when you're traveling uncharted roads with no real mentor or roadmap. I hadn't really developed my ability to hear God and distinguish his voice from mine or the devil. Today I mentor many gifted and anointed people, so they'll know how to embrace their giftings and how to deal with some of the rejection they're currently experiencing. It comes with the gift/job. One thing I stress is that people take time to see how God specifically deals with them. It may be vastly different than how he deals with someone else. He may deal with you one way in one season but another way in another season. I highly recommend "The Art of Hearing God" course by John Paul Jackson. Your life and ministry will depend on your ability to hear from God.

Over the years, I've learned that God will give me a word or scripture, and when I hear someone use that word or phrase, my spirit will come alive, and I'm supposed to stop and listen. At this point, I want to deal with a few lessons I learned and share them with you: Metanoia, Offense, Hesed, Righteousness, and Praise. Beware that rejection and criticism comes with every anointing and each level of grace you encounter.

Metanoia: Repentance (A Change or Renewing of your Mind)

God had spoken the word "Metanoia" in my spirit. I didn't know how to spell or pronounce it correctly, so I really couldn't look it up. I didn't know what it meant. It was in my spirit but not my head, so I didn't always remember it. Several years later, a bit frustrated because it was still an open issue in my life; while passing through the channels, I heard Pastor Joseph Prince (a newcomer to me) say "Metanoia." There it was. He had spoken the word that I'd been searching for years to find. I listened and my life has not been the same since. Metanoia is repentance; it means a change of mind, a change in thinking, not just tears and sorry. God wanted me to change the way I was thinking about the following topics: a) Offenses, b) Grace, c) Righteousness, and d) Praise. He was going to tweak my theology... My ducks in a row were going to be dismantled. Oh noooo... (Acts 19:1-8)

Metanoia – a baptism of repentance – immersion in repentance – change of mind.

It is the immersion of grace that enables you to be pliable (change, shift, turn) in the hands of God to move with whatever he does next. Otherwise, you stay stuck in what God did of old. It takes a special grace to slip out of tradition into the now will of God. (Bishop Clarence McClendon)

This teaching went along with what God had previously told me, "...I must have people (children) that will both hear and obey my word however it comes".

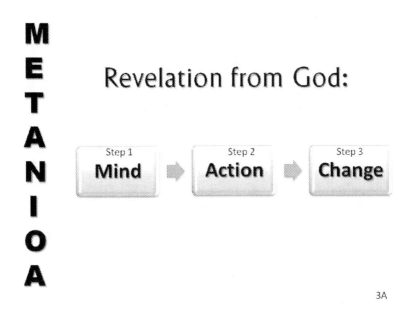

Revelation from God:

Step 1		Step 2		Step 3
Mind	⟹	**Action**	⟹	**Change**

3A

I've come to realize in life; all doctrine is incomplete. Between what I've learned and what I'm being taught is the truth, so I asked God to teach me. I want to know the truth. I go to the bible to find truth, not to prove I'm right;

those were God's instructions for me years ago. I was fascinated by how some people do nothing and get revelations while others fast and pray to get the same revelation. A well-known Pastor told about a revelation she'd gotten after a 21 day fast. I was interested in what she had to say. Then I spoke with my aunt and she told me she wanted to share something that the Lord had told her as she was walking down the hallway of her home. It was the same revelation. One fasted 21 days, and the other fasted for 0 days. Which is right? Both, but I believe we have been so ingrained in law we forget grace. That's why it's so important to learn how God deals with you and flow in that anointing.

Offenses:

God was preparing me for teachings that I would receive from ministers I'd written off.

I think the easiest people to offend are prideful people. I watched John Paul Jackson speak on the topic of offense. They talked about how being offended stops what God has called you to do. John Paul said, "When you go through prolong tests or trials, God is wanting you to change the way you think about something concerning your assignment, your appointment, and the enemy wants to stop that from happening. Ask the Lord to change your thinking (metanoia), commit your ways unto the Lord, and your thoughts will be established (recognize God's way in what you are doing) and make choices based on those new thoughts. You can't believe God if you are mad/offended at him. Don't get offended with God because of the way He does things: His timing, His method I thought He was going to do this, but He did that". Trust God to do everything for your good.

When you are too emotionally involved, your thoughts can be affected/skewed. If you trust God, you also have to trust his timing in your situation. I had several people I had to forgive and get over my offenses. Three, in particular, was such a blessing to me later in my life and ministry. The enemy sets us up by having us offended by people. If you're offended by someone, they can't effectively speak into your life. Don't expect to continue to receive from someone's anointing if you are offended with them.

Sin can make your witness ineffective and bring offenses to your listening audience. I saw ministers with such great anointings that were no longer effective because of sin in their past. God had forgiven them, but their influence and ability to speak into the lives of others had greatly been compromised. Also, there were those I just didn't care for their personalities, and there were those whose ministerial presentation was just not for me. Funny thing, God didn't care about how I felt, whether I was offended or not, when he wanted to teach or change me.

There were also people of my denomination that didn't support women preachers and made it hard for us as we pursued the things of God. I didn't call me to the ministry; God did.

Thinking about it now, I would never have called me. You would be shocked at some of the things people in ministerial leadership do behind the scenes. There were those who were in sin and wanted to pull me into their world, but I wasn't going for that, as my grandmother would say, "I could do bad all by myself."

When I first started ministry, God was always correcting me. It was aggravating, but I was young and not so wise. The initial leadership that rejected me, God would mend those fences (offenses) years later because that's the kind of God we serve. Bitterness, unforgiveness, envy, strife, or any negative emotions only stifle your walk with God and his ability to use you to your fullest potential. Forgiveness is more about freeing you than freeing the other person. Holding on to past hurts and injustices with hatred in your heart will only destroy you. I like the saying, "Unforgiveness is like taking poison, thinking the other person is going to die." It allows the enemy a foothold that can quickly become a stronghold in your life. Forgive and live and create new memories that are positive and not negative (hurtful/harmful).

Hesed – Grace

Lying on my bed, I saw in a vision the word "Heis." I thought it was "He Is" or maybe it is "He is the One and Only" my only source... I'd just told someone God doesn't speak in another language or a language you don't understand. I was wrong again (lol)... Another word that I didn't know its meaning, but this time I didn't wait years before I looked it up. I didn't get a lot of information on it. Again Joseph Prince to the rescue. This particular morning I set-up in bed, and while watching his program, he mentioned the word, Heis. Thinking again, God really has a sense of humor; now he's gonna teach me Greek about Grace.

1 Peter 5:10 -But the God of all grace, who hath called us unto his eternal glory by Christ Jesus, after that ye have suffered a while, make you perfect, stablish, strengthen, settle you.

John 1:16 - And of his fulness have all we received, and grace for grace.

Joseph Prince would teach on a new level of grace as it related to righteousness. He stated God is after heart transformation and not behavior modification. Only the grace of God can make that kind of change in our lives. I'm used to doing a lot of things, so the law wasn't so bad for me (all my ducks in a row), but what I missed out on was the more ducks, the more rituals, the less time and intimacy with God.

My relationship with God started out great. As time passed, the more I learned, the more things I had to do to please God, or so I thought. At first, I had a loving and carefree relationship with the Father, but when the list of do's and don'ts kept growing, I began to feel like I never quite measured up to his expectation. I began to think it was nicer when I knew less when it was just God and me and not the many man-made rules I'd learned.

I remember God waking me up one morning and talking to Him; it was so sweet, then I remembered that I had to go because I had to practice the presence of God as I'd learned. He said, "Rea, I'm already here." I still laugh about it. When you walk in law and not grace, you become hard like the Pharisees and Martha. When you walk by grace, you sit at the feet of Jesus and learn and enjoy his presence like Mary. When you're hard on yourself, you're probably hard on other people as well. Walking in grace helps you to be easier on yourself and others because you're trusting in the finished works of Christ and not the works of any man, including yourself.

Luke 10:40-42 - But Martha was cumbered about much serving, and came to him, and said, Lord, dost thou not care that my sister hath left me to serve alone? bid her therefore that she help me.

41 And Jesus answered and said unto her, Martha, Martha, thou art careful and troubled about many things:

42 But one thing is needful: and Mary hath chosen that good part, which shall not be taken away from her.

Grace: Hesed (defined)

- *Grace Undeserved and Unmerited Favor – Rom 5:17*
- *God's willingness to use His resources on our behalf (Grace) – 2Cor 8:9*
- *We don't get what we deserve; we get what Jesus deserve (awesome) – Gal 3:13-14*
- *God is my source, and everything else is a resource – Jas 1:17*
- *Grace is a person (Jesus Christ). He is Grace and Truth personified – John 1:17*
- *Righteousness is a gift of the Grace of God; it can't be earned – Phil – 1:11*

An intimate relationship with a Father that loves and cares for you may never be experienced by the child of God who's always trying to work to earn his love and acceptance. Even in works - "Rules without relationship leads to rebellion." (Josh McDowell) A God that is seen as harsh and uncaring is what many have been taught. Perfection or no Presence. I believe there are seasons when God removes all crutches from our lives and makes himself our only source without the usual resources. You can embrace it quickly and save yourself a lot of heartache and pain, or you can do it your way and arrived at your final destination looking like you were in a fight and everyone had a bat but you. Surrender now or Surrender later; it's your choice. (I should know)...

Isa 55:8-11- For my thoughts are not your thoughts, neither are your ways my ways, saith the Lord. For as the heavens are higher than the earth, so are my ways higher than your ways, and my thoughts than your thoughts. 10 For as the rain cometh down, and the snow from heaven, and returneth not thither, but watereth the earth, and maketh it bring forth and bud, that it may give seed to the sower, and bread to the eater: 11 So shall my word be that goeth forth out of my mouth: it shall not return unto me void, but it shall accomplish that which I please, and it shall prosper in the thing whereto I sent it.

Paradox

God sent other great ministers of the gospel to teach me on the subject of Grace. There are miles of difference between what I learned in the past and what I'm now being taught.

Being analytical has been both my best and worst quality. Best in that, I examine and test everything in line with the Word. Worst in that, in God, not everything is understandable or makes sense to the human mind; it must be accepted by faith alone. The basic premise God was teaching me was, "Just because I couldn't figure out a way, didn't mean God didn't have a way out." He was going to deal with me on a new and higher level concerning Grace. Sometimes when I'd figured everything out, He would interrupt my well-planned execution with "Hold off on that." It was up to me at that point to accept or reject his recommendation. I learned that the shortest distance between two points is a straight line, or in my case, God's way. When he said, "I got this" or "I'm here," that meant just what he said. You could go to bed and sleep at that point.

Deut 29:29 - The secret things belong unto the Lord our God: but those things which are revealed belong unto us and to our children forever, that we may do all the words of this law.

Bishop Clarence McClendon also did an excellent job teaching "Standing in Grace and Walking by Faith." Like the experience with Pastor Joseph Prince, I was lying in bed going through the channel when he came on and mentioned Metanoia. His teaching so inspired me that we entitled our Women's Conference that year "Standing in Grace." I learned so much about this new dimension of the Grace of God, but it also showed how legalistic I was. People must realize that no one person or body in Christ has all the revelation on a particular subject. Our walk with God is predicated on progressive revelation.

The more you walk with him, the more he will reveal his hidden treasures which demand shifts in our lives and teaching. God rarely tells his secrets to strangers. As I studied and embraced much of the grace teaching, I saw God do miracles when my back was against the wall, and I saw him do even greater works when I changed or realigned my plans with his. The gospel preached must be Christ-centered and not man. We look a lot better in Christ than standing alone. Righteousness has great perks.

When God wants to do a Shift, He sends a prophetic word. - McClendon

1) *Revelation from God of the new thing*
2) *God sends a prophetic word – Transformation*
3) *Shift – change our suddenlies of God*
4) *Change (On your mark, Get ready, Get set, Go (with it).*

The option of change is given to all men, but sad to say, many aren't ready for it. They want to live in the traditions of yesterday, rather than embracing what God is doing today. I believe every move should be tried and tested, as the scripture says, but we must be open to new revelations. In this place, we continually stand in the grace of God and walk victoriously by faith. Faith not in our ability to stand, but faith in the finished work of Jesus Christ: In Christ, in whom we have redemption. It is the place where impossibilities become realities. (1 Thess 5:21, Mark 7:13) A new revelation is not disrespect for the old but a season of change to embrace the new moves of God.

Righteousness is imputed by faith through Grace. Until you are secure in your stand in the Grace of God, you're never be able to walk by faith. Our righteousness is based on Christ's performance and perfection and not ours.

Steps in Grace:

- *We Stand Secure in the Grace of God (Righteousness – Once and for all)*
- *We Walk by Faith in the finished work of Christ Jesus (Salvation/Redemption)*
- *We Soar/Live in the Spirit by the Power of the Holy Spirit (Glorification)*

- *We are Hidden in Christ (Like pages in a book)*

We Stand Secure in the Grace of God (Righteousness – Once and for all)

Rom 5:1-2 - Therefore being justified (just if I never sinned) by faith, we have peace (nothing missing, nothing broken) with God through our Lord Jesus Christ: By whom also we have access by faith (substance, title deed) into this grace (undeserved, unmerited favor) wherein we stand, and rejoice in hope (earnest expectation of good) of the glory (manifested presence) of God.

This is the process that we have been made righteous in God when we receive Jesus as our Lord and Savior. It's not by works where we can boast. We don't lose our righteousness in God after salvation when we sin, but I believe that our relationship with God is strained because of guilt and condemnation when we miss the mark (sin). Like Matthew: the tax collector, the more I behold Jesus, the less I want to sin. (Rom 5:17, Eph 2:8-10, Rom 8:1)

We Walk by Faith in the finished work of Christ Jesus (Salvation/Redemption) – 2 Cor 5:7 - (For we walk by faith, not by sight)

Salvation is what we have in Christ and starts at the New Birth: when we accept Jesus as our personal Lord and Savior – Rom 10:9-10

- *The Plan of Salvation was God (Gen 3:15)*
- *Jesus took that Plan, took it to its ultimate completion: Hung, Bled, Died (Matt 26:28, John 19:30-34)*
- *God raised Jesus from the dead by the glory of God (Rom 6:4)*
- *Christ is revealed to us by the power of the Holy Ghost (1 Cor 2:10)*
- *We are then made the righteousness of God in Christ (2Cor 5:21)*

Many are waiting for God to do for them what he's already done in Christ. We are to stand in faith from the perspective of already having and not trying to obtain. Example: Sickness - I'm already healed in the mind of God; the enemy is trying to take what is lawfully mine. It is at that point I begin to declare God's healing word over me and give thanks for my healing until I see the manifestation of what I have spoken.

We Soar/Live in the Spirit by the Power of the Holy Spirit *(Glorification)-(2 Cor 3:18, Gal 5:22-25)*

Once we receive Christ as our LORD and Savior, our character is built on the foundation of the fruit of the Spirit, and without it, we are destined to fall. We take off the old man and put on the new man, which is not law-given, but spirit received by grace. This process operates in our lives as we renew our minds and transform our thinking and actions. We operate in the Power gifts as the Holy Spirit leads and anoints us. The Holy Spirit must build our character before we can truly and effectively walk in our gifts. Otherwise, our gifting without character will lead to abusive and destructive ways. Our flesh is tamed as the fruit of the Spirit is exercised. As we walk in the Spirit, we are changed into the image of God. We go from faith to faith and from glory to glory in Christ by the Spirit of God.

We are hidden in Christ *(like pages in a book) – He never changes.*

Col 3:1-4 - If ye then be risen with Christ, seek those things which are above, where Christ sitteth on the right hand of God.

2 Set your affection on things above, not on things on the earth.

3 For ye are dead, and your life is hid with Christ in God.

4 When Christ, who is our life, shall appear, then shall ye also appear with him in glory.

*God doesn't change; He is constant and stable. Because of this, we can stand secure in His grace, being made righteous once and for all. It's a done deal. I like the saying, "Grace, **God's** Riches (righteousness) **At Christ** Expense. Once we start believing right, we can begin to live right". Right believing produces Right living (Joseph Prince) – When you believe you are sealed in the Righteousness of Christ, new revelations given by God can then transform you.*

It's no small matter that people aren't changed and even alienated by those that bring new revelations to the church. We can only embrace those things we can identify with. If our identity is in Christ, when God wants to do a new thing, we will move with him and not remain stagnant with men's traditions and mindsets. God will not force you to change, but hint: It's to your advantage to surrender early. God is always right. (Mal 3:6, Rev 1:8)

- *Jesus Christ the same yesterday, and today, and forever. (Yeshua) - Heb 13:8*
- *Yahweh - Lord (God) – (is, was, is to come) - John 1:-1-5*

When the cloud moved in the Old Testament, the tribes moved, and when it stopped, they stopped. People who have received in one season are usually hesitant to move to the next season. They saw it work at that period in time, but time itself tells you something is wrong, something is old, it's no longer working, and it's time to move on to the new. God will give you the grace you need for the next level, but it's done by faith (faith cometh by hearing and hearing). Your heart must be opened to the next level and move of God, or you will become stagnant, stuck in a rut, and miss what God is wanting to do now. (Num 9:21-22, Rom 1:17)

Praise – Greater Glory (Presence, Power, and Goodness)

DOXOLOGY – Glory Word (a good opinion of God)

When times are hard - when you face the injustices of life. When you feel like a failure. When you wonder where's God in the midst of your circumstances. Does he really care? Why has he let this happen to me? When you have more questions than answers. In all of these situations, your mind and circumstances will challenge the very core of your belief system. You will become bitter or better depending on how you deal with the problem. Maintaining a good attitude during hard times is crucial. Many walk away from ministry, family, friends, and even God at this point. Hope is lost when you don't see any possibility of change for your good in your present dilemma. People aren't always supportive during your crisis.

I remember being so down that just getting out of bed and making it to church was all I could do. That was my sacrifice of praise. You never know the story behind a person's smile. That's the very reason we shouldn't sit in judgment of someone's praise. Man judges on the outward appearances, but God judges the heart of every matter. Listen to your spirit and not your head in difficult matters. (Prov 13:12, 1 Sam 16:7) Praise is one of the greatest weapons against Satan. (2 Chron 20:22, Ps 8:2)

After the initial shock of the test or trial, you must believe that God will work it out for your good. Through your tears, you must believe in "Hope" - Let it be your anchor - Hope that we both know and serve a God that can do anything but fail and that he is a Father that loves and cares for us. He has already made provision for our comeback. This trial is just stepping stones to our next level of victory. We go from victory to victory in every battle when we're in Christ. If you don't have any natural hope, go to the Word and get some supernatural hope from the promises of God. Be like father Abraham, who hoped against hope. (Rom 8:28, Ps 100:5)

When under attack, remember the following:

- *Watch your words and attitude because they can quickly become negative, and now you're battling God, yourself, and the enemy*
- *Get on God's side; when God saw darkness, He spoke "Light Be"... When Satan tempted Jesus, He said, "It is Written"... Speak Gods word until things change*
- *Sing praises to God Hint: If you can't praise God for your current circumstances, recount past victories and praise him until faith comes*
- *See yourself in the floodgates of God's love, grace, and mercy*
- *See yourself at an open door of access to the Father, The Ruler of the universe*
- *Surround yourself with people of like precious faith*
- *Be real with God and Ask for his help (Humble yourself under the mighty hand of God)*
- *Keep believing the Word (Logos, Rhema), Believe what you saw in the light (good time) is still true in the dark (bad times)*

- *Immediately change your words when you say something negative to something positive with no condemnation*
- *If what you see does not align itself with the word, then it's not over*
- *Say it until you See it…*
- *God gives his children songs in the night to help you through your storms (Ps 40:3)*
- *One Word from God can change anything and anybody (Mark 4:14-20).*

Even when times are bad, are hard, remember God is still good. Faith does not only believe God can; it's knowing God's willingness to help. Thank God trouble don't last always, and believe that there will be a brighter day ahead. Praise elevates you into the presence of God no matter what level of walk you're on in Christ. If Satan can't steal your joy, he can't have your goods (Jerry Savelle). My bad attitude hindered my altitude (my ability to move on). Therefore I was stuck in the same place of defeat until it changed. When I was struggling, I got the greatest release when I surrender everything to God; with the tag, there's nothing I can do about this, and I put it in your hands. Tell God: "You got mail."

God is so merciful. He will help you. I can recall countless nights when I felt helpless to do anything about my situation. It was in those moments God did the greatest miracles. It was never my ability to hold on to Him, but his ability to hold on to me. His hand is bigger and stronger; that's why praise is so important when you stand at the crossroads of life. Remember, when God inhabits your praises, He comes and brings gifts with him. Gifts of peace, prosperity, deliverance, healing, health, any and everything you need, want, or desire. Glory to God. Your faith will be tested at each level of growth, but it will hold. Hope will be an anchor to your soul if you put your faith in God and not yourself of your flaky emotions. Emotions have to be brought into submission, or you'll be on a perpetual roller coaster. Up and down, up and down until you're finally so down, you feel you can't ever get up again. When God doesn't do it your way, don't get discouraged, He has a better plan than you.

2 Cor 10:4-6 - (For the weapons of our warfare are not carnal, but mighty through God to the pulling down of strong holds;) 5 Casting down imaginations, and every high thing that exalteth itself against the knowledge of God, and bringing into captivity every thought to the obedience of Christ; 6 And having in a readiness to revenge all disobedience, when your obedience is fulfilled.

The lessons on Metanoia, Offense, Hesed, Righteousness, and Praise would be instrumental in equipping me for my new season and level with God. I couldn't go into my new season with this old baggage without compromising the new.

Matt 9:17- Neither do men put new wine into old bottles: else the bottles break, and the wine runneth out, and the bottles perish: but they put new wine into new bottles, and both are preserved.

Lessons Learned:

If what you see doesn't align itself with the word of God, then it's not over.

God has already done all he's going to do about any given situation or circumstance; it's up to us to receive what Christ has secured for us in grace.

Faith reaches into the world of the spirit, brings what we need into the natural realm, and is released by our words. Begin to speak the word of God over your situation.

God was teaching me that a Change (Metanoia) was coming about the subject of Hesed (Grace) and that in order to receive what God had for me, I had to change (shift) my way of thinking, which began with renewing my mind and ended with my praise. Grace focus is not on my doing, but what God has done in Christ and then my place in Christ called Righteous (being). It is indeed a walk of faith, so fight the good fight of faith without offense. Stand in grace, Walk by faith, and see God take you from victory to victory in Christ Jesus. Always remember God's love, grace, and mercy endure forever towards you.

"Just because I couldn't figure out a way didn't mean God didn't have a way out."

Declare: I am the Righteousness of God. Today will be a great day for me. I receive it by faith as I stand secure in God's grace and love". Amen

Prophetic Words:

Use your words to change your world, not your world to change your words...

A new revelation is not disrespect for the old but a season of change to embrace the new moves of God.

CHAPTER FOUR

DREAMS AND VISIONS

Scripture:

Acts 2:17-18 - And it shall come to pass in the last days, saith God, I will pour out of my Spirit upon all flesh: and your sons and your daughters shall prophesy, and your young men shall see visions, and your old men shall dream dreams:

18 And on my servants and on my handmaidens I will pour out in those days of my Spirit, and they shall prophesy:

Hab 2:2-3 - And the Lord answered me, and said, Write the vision, and make it plain upon tables, that he may run that readeth it.

3 For the vision is yet for an appointed time, but at the end it shall speak, and not lie: though it tarry, wait for it; because it will surely come, it will not tarry.

Story:

Dreams have often been described as the place where the subconscious meets the conscious. I've also heard it described as the place where God can have your undivided attention. For me, it's the place where the natural meets the supernatural. For years my sister and I argued about the meaning of our dreams. Little did I know that dreams can be literal (like mine) and symbolic (like hers). Because my dreams were mainly literal, it didn't take a lot of time or thinking to interpret them. They would be so accurate that it was like déjà vu when they occurred.

Some of my dreams were prophetic in nature others were personal activities that I would later encounter. Some were tormenting until I understood the symbolism in them. Even in literal dreams, there may be elements of symbolism. It is believed that all people dream, whether or not you remember them, is contributed to different factors. The more you value dreams, the more you will have them. If you de-value them, you remember them less. The frustrating things about dreams are they can be so vivid upon waking but lost as you began to prepare for your day. That's why it's so important that you take the time to write them when you first wake. You don't have to write a book, but enough to keep the dream in the forefront of your mind.

When recording a dream, I write and date the dreams initially and later format and interpret them. I've gotten up and recorded songs that I've been singing in my dreams. If I could only play an instrument to go along with them, I would make millions. God still meets us in our dreams as he did with men of old. Dream interpretation can be rewarding if done correctly. They can be used to warn, heal, enlighten, encourage, guide, and inform us in our day-to-day lives. (Dan 2:19, Gen 41:16)

When my dreams became more symbolic, I had to learn to interpret them. I've studied for years with various authors, but two that stand out for me are John Paul Jackson and Barbie Breathitt. I created my own personal dream dictionary with symbols that are strictly mine as well as what I've learned from books and other ministries. The most important thing about dream interpretation is asking the Holy Spirit to help you interpret all dreams.

Be sure to leave room for error and lessons learned, especially when you're interpreting someone else's dreams. Many times they may leave things out that can totally alter the entire dream. I've met people who wanted me to almost tell them what they've dreamed rather than telling me their dream and having me interpret it for them. I usually don't bother; you have to be open and cooperative with the dream interpreter. Only God can give you a dream that has been forgotten or hidden by the dreamer. It's exciting to see the plans of God, Satan and man revealed through dreams and visions.

Dreams and visions are recorded in both the Old and New Testaments. Joel and the Apostle Paul record these prophetic encounters, and they are available to us for guidance and help. For the closed-minded, maybe God is trying to tell you something through dreams and vision. Stay open and judge everything by the Word of God. (Acts 2:17-18, Joel 2:28-29)

The Bible record dreams throughout the creation of time. God speaks to the saint and sinner via dreams. Today many people don't take time to appreciate how important dreams can be in one's life. It's funny; they will read scriptures about dreams and accept them as truth and worthy of being read but give no thought to their own dreams. Recurring dreams are important because they reflect the concept that there are unfinished things in your life that should be addressed.

Biblical Dreams:

> - *Abimelech – Gen 20:3 (Sarah, Abraham's wife)*
> - *Jacob – Gen 28:12-13 (A ladder to heaven: angels ascending and descending)*
> - *Laban – Gen 31:24 (Speaking to Jacob neither good nor bad)*
> - *Joseph – Gen 37 (Future Rulership)*
> - *Baker and Butler - Gen 40 (Life and Death) - Joseph Interprets*
> - *Pharaoh – Gen 41 (Coming Famine) – Joseph Interprets*
> - *Solomon – 1King 3:5 (God said, Ask what I shall give thee)*
> - *Nebuchadnezzar – Dan 2 (Great Image) – Daniel Tells and Interprets*
> - *Belshazzar – Dan 4 (A tree in the midst of the earth) - Daniel Interprets*
> - *Joseph– Mat 1:20, Mat 2:12-19 (Concerning Jesus)*

DREAMS TYPES:

Prophetic dreams: Are given to a person by God, representing what the Father is about to do or is doing in a given situation.

Literal Dreams: Are dreams where the incident occurs literally, as it is shown in the dream – It comes past just as I'd seen it.

Symbolic Dreams: Are dreams where one object is represented by another object.

Recurring Dreams: Are dreams that are dreamed more than once, usually with additional information in each dream. These usually occur because closure has not been obtained in the previous dream.

Misinterpretation of a Dream: A wrong interpretation of a dream. Evaluate where you missed it and keep it moving.

Visions are a sure thing to happen. If they are from God in the form of a promise, they may be greatly tested, but hold on to them until they come to pass.

There's a world of the spirit that we can tap into that makes our lives fun and exciting. It can warn and correct things in our lives because these actions are often orchestrated by God. It's of utmost importance that we ask the Holy Spirit to assist us in the interpretation of dreams. Dreams can be tricky. As great as books are, the interpretations of symbols can be altered by a variety of things that relate to the individual person. Most symbols have a dual meaning: the color green can mean growing or envious.

Anybody can say they had a dream about something after the manifestation. I share my dreams with trusted family and friends before the event happens. I share for two reasons. 1) To obtain a witness 2) Check the accuracy of my ability to hear and understand my dreams.

In conclusion, God speaks to His children in various ways. Hearing the voice of God and knowing the heart of the Father will provide adventure and exploits for those who would desire to be used in this season. Be careful to be led by the Holy Spirit when you're interpreting dreams.

Now take the plunge and start to pay attention to your dream and start recording them. When you're really comfortable, you might even interpret them for others. Have Fun…

Welcome to the Supernatural World of Dreams and Visions.

Below is a format I use to record my dreams.

DREAM RECORDING

- ❏ *Write/Record your dream (Title and Date Dream)*
  Include Actions, Feelings, Settings, People, Colors, Symbols (Items)
- ❏ *Ask the Holy Spirit to give you the interpretation*
- ❏ *Ask the Holy Spirit to help you recall a dream if you've forgotten the dream*
- ❏ *Use dream dictionary interpretation to identify symbols*
- ❏ *Identify Literal vs. Symbolic dreams*
- ❏ *Identify Prophetic vs. Personal Dreams*
- ❏ *Recurring dreams (unfinished situations – important in nature)*
- ❏ *Keep a personal dream dictionary of words and associations (direction: new place)*
- ❏ *Revisit your dreams for accuracy*
- ❏ *Take dream courses (John Paul Jackson, Barbie Breathitt)*

Dream (Date) _____

Dream:

_____

_____

_____

Symbols & Interpretation:

_____

_____

_____

My Interpretation:

_____

_____

_____

Comments:

_____

_____

_____

Sample:

Dream: Bus out of Control (Personal, Symbolic)

Dream: I dreamed that I was on a bus. <u>The bus was going out of control</u>. I was trying to steer it. I woke the driver up. <u>He had fallen asleep</u>. He put his foot on the brake. I was looking for my son. He had gotten lost. I'd seen this other little boy from the back. I thought it was my son, but it wasn't. As the bus was moving, I looked out of the window, and I saw my son and another little boy walking down the street. I thought he was still on the bus. I had the bus driver stop and turned around. <u>We went back to get my son</u>. I called his name "SJ." My son looked just like the little boy that was in my last dream. When I called him, he knew his name and stopped to wait for me to come back and get him.

Interpreter: (DM)

Interpretation: You feel like portions of your life are out of control, and some relationships are out of place. <u>Perhaps you feel like God doesn't care, as if He is asleep at the wheel of your life. You have tried to fix things yourself only to find out that it only leads to frustration.</u> This dream reminds you that God is in control. <u>He will restore the disconnected relationships in your life.</u>

Symbols:

Life (areas) out of control - God — is asleep at the wheel of my life

Trying to steer it (Fix it myself, don't understand it – Yes Lord, Yes)

Restoration – went back to get my son

Driver (God) - Wakes up (becomes involve, he hears my prayer)

* Note if you can't see a person, usually it's the Holy Spirit or some angelic being

Interpreter: Rena M Wilburn

Areas of my life are out of control.

Comment: Rena

I know that God knows and hears, but I was questioning when He will restore and give me Restitution for my losses?

Lessons Learned:

All dream interpretations and visions should be prayed over, and as we allow the Holy Spirit to lead and guide us, they will be of great benefit to the dreamer and those who the dream content shall impact. I like what Dr. V. Raymond Edman said, "Never doubt in the darkness what God has shown you in the light." Dream Big, God can handle it.

Remember: Emotions and familiarity of the dreamer can affect your ability to interpret a dream. Stay neutral; just read the symbols (signs) and ask the Holy Spirit for his assistance.

Prophetic Words:

The value of the dream is determined by the source or giver of the dream. Watch out for Dream Killers and Vision Stealers.

CHAPTER FIVE

SPEAK LORD

Scripture:

1 Sam 3:9-10 - Therefore Eli said unto Samuel, Go, lie down: and it shall be, if he call thee, that thou shalt say, <u>Speak, Lord; for thy servant heareth</u>. So Samuel went and lay down in his place.

10 And the Lord came, and stood, and called as at other times, Samuel, Samuel. Then Samuel answered, Speak; for thy servant heareth.

Ezek 12:25 - For I am the Lord: I will speak, and the word that I shall speak shall come to pass; it shall be no more prolonged: for in your days...

John 6:63- It is the spirit that quickeneth; the flesh profiteth nothing: the words that I (Jesus) speak unto you, they are spirit, and they are life.

Story:

Learning how God communicates with you will be one of the most important things you will learn as you travel through this lifetime. One of the most interesting and sometimes frustrating things is that God is progressive, and when we settle on a certain method, he'll change on you. Learning how the enemy deals with you is also important because many battles are lost in his counterattacks. The ability to hear God in this day and time is a matter of life or death. Choose Life. (Eph 5:15-17, Deut 30:19) Many times I would ask God, "Quite my spirit that I might hear your voice."

God uses different methods to communicate his word, thoughts, will, and ways. I believe many people make the mistake of believing that the only method He uses is the method he uses with them. I can present to you the methods for which I'm accustomed, but the reality of it all is that you have to know how God expresses himself to you and be open to new and progressive change. Below are the ways He uses to communicate with me: a) Dreams & Visions b) Prophetic Words c) Prophetic Anointings d) Power Gifts or e) a combination of any of these. (Isa 55:8, 1 Cor 2:9-10)

I. Dreams & Visions:

As a small child, God primarily used dreams to communicate with me.

Dream: *I remember very vividly a dream of seeing a city of lights coming down from heaven. I was thoroughly confused because I'd only been taught when we die, we went up to heaven. I didn't know one day, heaven would come to earth. Thinking I was so far off, I didn't share it with anyone because people already thought I was a little weird, or at least they made me feel that way.*

Vision: *My sister and her husband were out looking to purchase a car. While sitting outside on the porch, I see a vision of a light color car with a spoiler on it. Later as I look up from reading my book, there they were driving down my street in their new car they'd just found. They'd driven it over to show me, it was light beige, but it didn't have a spoiler. I asked where's the spoiler, and she said they ordered it. It didn't come with the car, but my brother-in-law wanted one, so they ordered it.*

Vision is my favorite method because it doesn't take much involvement on my part. A picture is worth a thousand words. (Rev 21:1-4)

II. Prophetic Words:

Upon opening my mouth, words would just flow. I was amazed, but without teaching, I thought it was just something nice that happened to everybody. Never did I think they had biblical meaning or consequences. Thinking back, those words I received from God always got me out of trouble or made me look good or smarter than I was. I learned early evil thoughts or harmful words against someone could, unfortunately, come to pass also, so I was careful what I said. Evil words happened more quickly than good but isn't that how Satan works? (2 Cor 10:4-5, Luke 12:11-12)

Just as God was teaching me how to hear his voice, the enemy began tormenting me. I found myself struggling to wake from sleep. I couldn't open my eyes, but I could hear what was going on around me. It was a horrible feeling. It was as if a presence would overshadow me. As a child, I hated naps during the day because I would be tormented if I was up late at night. My family tried to help by telling me to put matches in the form of a cross in my head, but that stuff didn't work. When I started studying the scriptures, I learned praise was a formidable weapon against the enemy. I praised God through the ordeal, and they became shorter and less frequent. However, it was still a battle. The enemy didn't want me; he wanted my gifting. I believe God gives a man a gift, but it's his choice to whom he will yield that gift, for good or evil. (Rom 11:29, Ps 8:2)

After being baptized in the Holy Ghost (praying in tongues), I learned this gift was also a powerful weapon against the enemy. When I prayed in the spirit, the Holy Spirit taught me things beyond my intellect. Moving in the Spirit, I knew when demonic forces were present before an attack. When those tormenting spirits came, I just said, "Holy Spirit, please protect me," and that was the end of that. The battle was over before it began. (John 14:26, 1 Peter 5:8-9)

The Next Phase was God speaking to me as I read scriptures. I believe it's his favorite way of communicating with me. It always took me longer than my friends when I studied or read anointed books because I took notes as the Holy Spirit spoke. This got a little expensive because no one wants you writing in their books, so I couldn't borrow theirs. It was as if the Holy Spirit would sit on my shoulder and guide me through each book from start to finish, but only as I invited him into my studies. Once, he led me to read the same verse for a week (Psalms 23:1). He was crucifying my flesh from the need to hurry and finish a chapter. I didn't know you could get so much out of one verse until then. It wasn't in the abundance of my reading but my comprehension and understanding that He was concerned about. (John 5:39, Prov 4:20-23)

I love memorizing scriptures, but my reasons weren't always the best at first. I sometimes used them against people to win senseless word battles. The scriptures I'd memorized were only in my head (intellect), not in my heart (spirit). Until the Word of God is in your heart, Satan can defeat you. One day when threatened by the enemy, I couldn't think of one scripture. When the Word of God became a part of me, in my heart, things changed. I didn't have to think of words to say; they would come up out of my spirit as weapons against the enemy. Now that's awesome. (Prov 20:27, 2 Cor 10:4-5)

I remember God telling me once concerning his people, "They can't see me, for you." It was hard but true, and I knew I had to make adjustments in my words, mostly my delivery. The words were correct, but they lacked the compassion hurting people needed. Many times the world judges God by his children. We are representatives, ambassadors with flaws; our words must display the love of the Father with compassion, love, hope, and kindness as well as direction and guidance in a particular area. Unfortunately, some lessons of compassion were learned by the things I suffered. They're the ones forever etched in my mind and in my heart. No one can minister with passion and compassion like someone who has been through what you're going through. (Col 4:6) God told me once to "Say it like He Said it, See it like He Sees it"...

Knowing the importance of the word, I set out to read the entire bible from Genesis to Revelation in different versions. Never in my wildest imagination did I dream God would show up to escort me through the scriptures. It was and is to this day a place I meet God in His Word. I was privileged to speak on one of my Overseers (Bishop J.L. Tyson) radio program on the subject "The Importance of the Word." He was and is such an encouragement to me.

The year through the bible method didn't work for me, but it works well for others.

I read as much as I was led at that particular time. The first version of the bible I read completely was "The Book." As a baby Christian, I would sit on the couch with a glass of wine and read the bible. God would talk to me as I read his Word.

I'm amazed at the number of Christians who fight for the right to read the bible and haven't read it through to know what's in it. The bible is the Christian owner's manual everything you ever need is in it. I thought the wine would relax me from a hard day at work. I really didn't drink it, and I kept thinking it was a waste of time even to pour it. When I was almost finished reading "The Book", God said, "You don't need that." I said, "Oh, okay." I would have thought he would have corrected me upfront, but he didn't. I was a babe in Christ, but I knew there was much more than what I've been taught because I'd experienced some supernatural encounters already. (2 Tim 2:15, Col 3:16)

III. Prophetic Anointing:

God began telling me things about people and situations I couldn't have known in the natural. People began to ask me to pray about certain situations in their lives and see what God had to say. I told them if he tells me, I'll tell you. Once someone asked me not to pray about something concerning them, and to this day, I don't get revelations about them anymore, even if they ask. I struggled with this phase because I wasn't always sure; is it God, is it me, or is it the Devil. It's in those moments I had to know the character of God (via his Word and Spirit) to know who's speaking. I had to trust my heart and let the peace of God rule when making my choices or decisions. (Col 3:15, Ps 103:7, Deut 29:29) I believed, if I asked God in humbleness of heart, he wouldn't let me go astray. People are quick to say you are a false prophet if you miss it.

Be prepared to miss it, to make mistakes as you are learning and being taught the things of God. Don't get discouraged and give up. You'll get more and more accurate and detailed as you walk with him. However, watch out for consistent errors, as the bible calls it's the spirit of error. God rarely tells his secrets to strangers. He meets you at the place where your heart looks for him. In this dispensation of grace, fellowshipping with God isn't as hard as most people try to make it. Just call on his name, then wait for him to speak or act on your behalf. (1 John 4:6, 1 Cor 2:9-16)

John 4:24 - God is a Spirit: and they that worship him must worship him in <u>spirit and in truth</u>.

With the word and the prophetic anointing working in harmony, I could search the heart of God. In difficult situations in my own personal life, I asked other anointed people to pray for and with me as confirmation of what I believed God was saying. The prophetic gifts and anointings are another mighty fortress against the enemy.

It's important that we always remember, it's God at work in us and not to touch His glory. Gifts and miracles are for the good of man and the glory of God. Every thought, dream, or vision must be interpreted in line with the Word and Spirit of God if you want truth and accuracy. Every God-given gift must be wrapped in humility, or one day it'll be wrapped in humiliation. (Isaiah 42:8, Acts 9:31)

The anointing of God originates from the heart of God; however, it can affect your natural senses. Caution: If the enemy can hold you in the natural realm, he can defeat you, but if you hold him in the faith realm, you can defeat him. (Kenneth E. Hagin) Your enemy has been defeated, but he's an outlaw, and his defeat must be enforced by faith.

Listed are examples of how the anointing of the Holy Spirit affected my natural senses:

Seeing: Dreams and Vision:

I see a young lady in the church hallway; I see her lungs; later that day, one of her lungs collapsed

A young girl at church passes in front of me; I see her with a high fever. The following Sunday, her mom stood in tears to tell how her daughter had had a dangerously high fever and could have died

I dreamed of a lady in a morgue; she is headless; I learned later she has developed severe mental problems

A young lady asked me to pray for her brother; I told her what I saw. I could tell she didn't like what I said. Later she told me she didn't tell him but that it happened just as I'd told her.

Sometimes I can change the things I see, but unfortunately, sometimes, I can't. I do my part and let God do his. He sees the whole picture, the unknown, and the things that hinder us from receiving. Never judge the right ways of man against the righteousness of God.

Hearing:

God's Voice - *"I got this, I'm here" or some other prophetic impartation or Scripture.*

When God says, "I got this"- it's a done deal, it's finished, and I could go to bed. God calls me "Rea" when he calls me Rena; I'm usually in trouble.

Man's voice - *I'll hear people's conversations, sometimes about me. It's funny to hear my name called in the spirit.*

I heard in my spirit, a friend of mine call my name. I didn't think any more of it, then my friend came over later that day, and I told her what I'd heard. She said that she was in his office and that he said he was going to call me.

Satanic voice - *Threatening or Condemning: Things like I'm going to kill you or I thought you were a Christian (when I missed it), It contradicts the Word or promises of God: Lies (It ain't gonna work this time).*

Note: The enemy will entice you to do wrong and condemn you when you do. Rebuke the Words and replace them with God's Word as a confession.

Demonic voices - *Babblings and statements like "You are dumb" or profanity and vulgarity."*

Touch:

Touching the hand of a lady, immediately I'm standing in her house describing to her what I see, she's amazed.

Using anointing oil as I pray for people in a healing line, I dipped the tip of my finger in the oil; suddenly, my hand is saturated with oil, but from where? It's not dripping on the floor.

Once I felt a light steady breeze over my face. After it was over, I look around, but there were no fans, no windows or doors open. It was a feeling of such peace that I so desperately needed at the time.

Touching people, I received personal revelations about them. I had to learn when and how to share those revelations. Some things should be spoken in private (learned that the hard way) whenever possible. It's more important to help people by not sharing their personal business with everybody than to try to impress others that you're gifted.

Taste:

Lying in bed, I started to taste anointing oil. I knew the smell. It was the oddest feeling. The taste kept getting stronger and stronger until it was no longer palatable and became overwhelming. (Rev 10:9-10)

Smell:

Godly: Pleasant, fresh flowers, sweet, etc.

Demonic: Unpleasant, foul

IV. Power Gifts:

1) *God said, "Go tell that pastor …" I didn't want to do it (fear of rejection again), but I did, and God blessed me. When the Pastor confirmed what I'd said, I was ecstatic and relieved.*
2) *I walked into my friend's church, immediately I told her, I see three figures. She tells me the person who ministered last night spoke on the Trinity.*
3) *Interpreting Tongues: I dream I'm quoting Psalms 23 verse by verse. A verse in English, the same verse in Tongues.*

A young lady began to speak in tongues; I wasn't really listening because the church hadn't embraced the Baptism of the Holy Ghost with the evidence of speaking in tongues. When God told me to stand and interpret, I had to confess; I wasn't listening. He told me a second time, so I stood strictly out of obedience. The truth about it was, hearing her wouldn't have mattered. I wasn't going to interpret the message; the Holy Spirit was. After I finished, someone stood to confirm that the speaker had spoken on that subject the night before. Whew… (1 Cor 14:14-15, 1 Cor 14:5)

I flow better in this anointing when there's anointed music. I thought that was strange until I read about the prophet Elisha (2King 3:15). I was in good company and felt better. There's nothing like praise and worship to propel you into the presence of the Lord. The scriptures say that God inhabits the praises of his people. My passion is to mentor people, especially young adults and children, with these gifts so they won't feel so out of place (as I did when I was their age). The more you walk in the anointing, the stronger your anointing will become.

Mentoring and grooming others to pass the baton is extremely important for the next generation. I received great teachings and partnerships from TV ministries to replace the lack of mentorship in my life, but of course, the Holy Spirit is the best teacher. My slight rebellious and know it all attitude didn't help. I had a heart for God and to see his children walk in victory, but I had to be trained so that my delivery matched my passion. It wasn't easy because I was easily offended when people didn't accept my word or calling, which stemmed from earlier rejection from leadership and family. I learned many things the hard way, but I learned them none-the-less. An attitude of gratitude (humbleness of heart) towards God and compassion towards man will take you far in the things of God and lead you to quicker and sustain victories. (2 Kings 3:14-15, Ps 22:3, 1 Tim 1:2)

When the Spirit is moving within me, or my spirit is excited or becomes alerted to something happening in the atmosphere, I usually get chills. However, one night while sitting at my computer, chatting with a friend, there was a force so great that I was physically moved almost out of my chair. I knew something had shifted in the atmosphere. Later I learned that a catastrophe had happened in Japan. You don't have to be present at a given place to know what's going on in that place. (1 Cor 5:3, 2 Kings 5:26)

Standing in church one Sunday, the Holy Spirit said, go and pray with the pastor's wife. Initially, I was hesitant; I didn't want to go because she had rejected something I said before. It had come true nonetheless. I guess I was still a little offended, but I needed to get over it. Suddenly I felt as if someone put their hand in my back and gently pushed me forward. He didn't have to tell me again. She'd been sick and wanted to go to the altar but didn't have the strength to get up and go, so I took her. (James 3:2, Rom 15:1)

IV. Finally: **Combinations (However it comes...)**

God spoke, "Rena, the time is short, and I must have people (children) that will both hear and obey my word however it comes. I took a Course "The Art of Hearing God" by John Paul Jackson, which I highly recommend to every person in ministry. He explains that God will build your character before he builds your ministry so that your gifting won't destroy you. Your character will protect you from your ego and the humiliation of being de-throne from the kingdoms we set up for ourselves, thinking higher of ourselves than we ought. Humbleness vs. Humiliation (Rom 12:3, 1 Cor 9:27)

God can use whatever method he chooses to communicate with us. Our part is to live in love, stand in grace, and walk by faith. As we do, we'll hear Him whisper His secrets to our hearts. We'll hear Him say, "This is the way; walk in it." God is speaking. Are you listening? (Isa 30:2, John 6:63)

Whether it's a Dream or Vision, Prophetic Word (Logos, Rhema), Scripture, Another person, even a life circumstance, take time to listen when God speaks, it's for your good, the good of others, and it brings glory to God. (Rom 8:28)

God Speaks

Previously we discussed how God speaks to me. Now let's address the issue of how we speak to God. First of all, let's establish that the word of God is the will of God for us on the earth. We are admonished to look not at the things which are seen for they are temporary (subject to change), but we are to look at that which is not seen, for they are eternal. We are to look to Jesus in every situation we face. He is the author and finisher of faith.

Our victory was won at Calvary, and we must see ourselves enforcing that word by fighting the good fight of faith while we stand in grace and walk by faith. (Note: faith only works by love Gal 5:6). When you're not walking in love, you're out-of-order. (Heb 12:2)

2 Cor 4:18 - For we look not at the things which are seen, but at the things which are not seen: for the things which are seen are temporal; but the things which are not seen are eternal.

Our words define our faith. Many times we will have to continually declare what is presently unseen until it's seen. Negative speaking or No speaking will produce after its own kind. There's absolutely nothing like receiving a word from the Lord in a given situation to bring things in alignment with the will of God. You must continue to declare that word in the midst of every obstacle,

51

every trial, until the gates of hell have to loose and let go whatever you are declaring unlawfully obtained. (Rom 10:6, Matt 16:19)

Positive words alone may not get the job done either, but the all-powerful word of the living God, revealed by the Spirit of God, is an assurance of victory in any given situation. Does it take great faith? The bible says the faith of a grain of mustard seed can move mountains (troubles). For years I thought I had to do this and that to get God to move, then I learned that God had already moved in Christ. Our words reach into the spiritual realm and 1) Take what has been appropriated by Christ and promised by covenant through faith 2) Bring into the natural realm (earth) the desired promise/result. Our faith must rest in the faithfulness and integrity of God's word. Take God at His word and stand on it (having done all, stand) – (Eph 6:13)

Matt 17:20 - And Jesus said unto them, Because of your unbelief: for verily I say unto you, If ye have faith as a grain of mustard seed, ye shall say unto this mountain, Remove hence to yonder place; and it shall remove, and nothing shall be impossible unto you.

Act on God's Word

When I acted on God's word and not my own ability, I saw results beyond my wildest imagination. My faith was no longer in my ability to hold on to God's unchanging hand, but it was in God's ability to hold on to my unstable hand. The hand of a God (Creator of the Universe) that can do anything but fail would assure me victory. The scripture says to "Have faith in God", not one's self. When you come to the end of your rope, your road, your ability to produce desired results, don't give up because it's only the end of man and the beginning of God's supernatural power. Stand on the Word… God will take you from victory to victory because He's that kind of God and Father, and most importantly, He so loves you, and his word is based on his covenant with you through the blood of Jesus.

We have his word for it. Many people today ask, What Will Jesus Do? I say he will do What the Word Says Do. (Ps 91:14-16)

Mark 11:22 - And Jesus answering saith unto them, Have faith in God.

When we have God's word on a subject, we can enter into rest. He told me one morning recently, in peace, he has established us. Remembering when David and I were trying to have a child. We'd been married for seven years, but we'd only start trying to have a child the last four. I'd gone to an infertility specialist with no positive results. I was so down and depressed because it had been four long, disappointing years. It looked hopeless, but God had already spoken, and I needed to trust him to make it good. Unfortunately, I was a long way from the rest of God. People told me we should adopt, but David wasn't hearing that. The chances of getting pregnant without medication were against us.

I tried infertility pills for about a week but stopped because I didn't want multiple births. I told the doctor I didn't want a liter taking those pills. When I told him God was going to give me a child, he all but laughed in my face. I stopped the visits and got rid of all the stress about having kids. It was too much for me. I needed a real vacation, I needed rest, and I needed time with God stress-free. When I'm at peace, I hear God clearer. The cares of life will choke the Word out of you and prevent you from communicating with him. Protect your peace at all cost. Heb 4:3 - For we which have believed do enter into rest.

My friend and mentor Barb (Neville) was planning a trip to Israel. When Charlene (Green) asked if I was going with them, Barb spoke up and said, yeah, she's going. I didn't have the money, but Barb had spoken, and so it was off to Israel. What a great decision she made for me. It was a time of great rest and peace. I needed to connect with my Father God and other saints with like precious faith. Israel is such a wonderful place to visit and discover your roots as a Christian. I walked where Jesus walked, and the sites make the bible all the more real.

As soon as I returned home, I got pregnant but didn't know it until I was 6½ months. I started dreaming about kids and saw this little girl in a yellow dress. I thought I was supposed to start teaching Sunday school. Never thinking I was pregnant, I began to have a few female problems: no morning sickness, no real weight gain. I was scheduled for an additional test because my doctor thought I had a cyst on my pituitary gland. Upon arriving for the x-rays, I told the nurse; I thought I might be pregnant. So she canceled the appointment and rescheduled the visit because he was out of town.

When my doctor examined me, he said, you're 26 weeks pregnant; I couldn't figure out at the moment how many months that was. He thought I was in shock. Now, who was laughing? He'd missed it on my previous exam. When I told people I was 6½ months, they would always say, you mean 6 ½ weeks. Then I would laugh and correct them no months, not weeks. We all laughed. God had proven himself faithful even when I was faithless. I needed to act on the word God had already spoken to me.

Kristin is a testimony of the faithfulness of God and the fact that God keeps his word and promises. He still does miracles. She has the same anointing, or I should say a stronger anointing than me. It's a generational gift and blessing. My grandmother, my mom, me, my sisters, and now my daughter with the same prophetic gift. Ain't God good? (2 Cor 1:20, Heb 10:23)

When God breathed into man the breath of life, man became a living (speaking) being. God has given us dominion and power to use the name of Jesus to declare and bring all things into alignment with His will and word. The believer's authority was bought, paid for, and sealed in the blood of Jesus, and it's available to all that enter in. When God saw darkness, he spoke light, and light has continued since he spoke it. God instructs us to speak as he has spoken. God said "yes" to us having a child, while the world said, "no". I had to stay in agreement with God even through my tears and little faith, but God was faithful, and Kristin is a constant reminder of his love and faithfulness. No one's "no" can compete with God's "yes". (Gen 2:7, Mark 16:17-20) - Believe it and Speak it.

2 Cor 4:13 - We having the same spirit of faith, according as it is written, I believed, and therefore have I spoken; we also believe, and therefore speak;

Lessons Learned:

God has already moved in Christ. Our part is to now receive what he'd accomplished

The ability to hear God in this day and time is a matter of life or death. Choose Life

Praise is a formidable weapon against the enemy

The anointing is supernatural, but it can affect your natural senses

God meets you at the place where your heart looks for him

Every God-given gift must be wrapped in humility, or one day it'll be wrapped in humiliation

If the enemy can hold you in the natural realm, he can defeat you, but if you hold him in the faith realm, you can enforce his Calvary defeat. Some things we can change in the spirit, other things we can't. God's gifts are for His glory and the good of all mankind.

Our words must show the love of God and His compassion towards mankind to be effective.

God told me once to "Say it like He Said it, See it like He Sees it." – He doesn't see you sick, He sees you healed - So say it.

Caution:

If the enemy can hold you in the natural realm, he can defeat you, but if you hold him in the faith realm, you can enforce his Calvary defeat.

Some things we can change in the spirit, other things we can't. God's gifts are for his glory and the good of all mankind. – Trust God to make the final decision for everybody's good.

When God is prophetically speaking through his servant, it's best to be quiet until the word is complete. Many times the word is lost or not heard because of the shouts of jubilee while the word is being given.

THE SUPERNATURAL: THE PLACE I MEET GOD
Speak Lord

Prophetic Words:

Until the Word of God is in your heart, Satan can defeat you

God is more concerned about your character than your ministry

The gifts of God are weapons against the enemy. Use them by speaking them forth.

CHAPTER SIX

THE SUPERNATURAL: THE PLACE
I MEET GOD (ELOHIM)

Scripture:

Dan 11:32 - And such as do wickedly against the covenant shall he corrupt by flatteries: but the people that do know their God shall be strong, and do exploits.

Story:

The SuperNatural: Rhema Word

The Supernatural is the place where the Natural meets the Spiritual. In many cases, it's a place where good meets evil: light meets darkness. The darkness will give way to the light because the light is the greater force when acted upon (God is light). It's the place I meet the Creator of the universe, and He tells me He loves me. It is in these moments He tells me the secrets of life (the prophetic). Shifting occurs when I meet God. It's the place where impossible things become possible and highly probable. (John 1:1-5, Luke 11:13)

Matt 19:26 - But Jesus beheld them, and said unto them, with men this is impossible, but with God all things are possible.

Who is this God? He is known in Genesis 1:1 as Elohim. Elohim is the plural of El and is the first name given for God in the Old Testament. In the traditional

THE SUPERNATURAL: THE PLACE I MEET GOD

The SuperNatural: The Place I Meet God (Elohim)

Jewish Elohim is the name of God as Creator and Judge of the universe. The names of God are powerful in of itself. I meet with the Creator of the Universe, and more importantly, He meets with me. To get a more exhaustive look at the names of God, visit Hebrews for Christians: (https://www.hebrew4christians.com/index.html) website.

Gen 1:1 - In the beginning, God (Elohim) created the heavens and the earth

God is awesome, and His ability to communicate with man is beyond comprehension. He stands outside of what we know as time and orchestrates our lives. He knows the end from the beginning. He's Omniscience. He knows everything about us, yet he has chosen to love us anyway. He waits for the invitation to come and make his home in us. It's an awesome experience when God and man are one. Shifting happens when we are one with the Creator. (Matt 10:8, Mark 16:17-20)

The Supernatural is a special place where miracles happen. It's the place where prayers are answered, and dreams are fulfilled. It's the realm where God and man are one and nothing; absolutely nothing is impossible.

The natural man takes off his natural and puts on the supernatural power of God. It's a place where time and space are defied and of no consequence. It's a place of peace from the loud noises of our everyday existence. The voice of the Lord is clear, and his heart is revealed. It's a place where you can really be you, flaws and all. Come in, take off your shoes and rest in His arms of love or sit at his feet and listen as he speaks to your heart, things you long to hear: It's a place where he heals you, delivers you, and fellowships with you. What a place to be - What a God?

When I'm in a real battle, the voice of God is so comforting and assuring. I've learned after I've made my request known through supplication, prayer, praise, and thanksgiving, I watch to hear what He will say to me. The story I'm about to share is an example of hearing God's voice and then watching him act on my behalf.

Scarlet Fever – "I'm Here"

My daughter (Kristin) battled with asthma as a child, and I believe every kind of strep. Back and forth to the doctor. Thank God she had a God-fearing doctor (Dr. Billye Jameson). Dr. Jameson was my best friend and mentor (Barb's) daughter. That in of itself was such a relief. She was in great hands both spiritually and physically. Secret: She even made a house call one day to check on Kristin. What a great friend!

Kristin would get fevers so high that it would heat the entire bed. During one of those fever episodes, she'd contracted Scarlet fever. She was as red as a tomato. Scarlet fever is a form of strep, and after three days, she was no longer contagious. However, people didn't know that, and they didn't want her around. That was okay because that became mother-daughter time. With prayer and medication, she was healed.

Another morning I woke up, and guess what, another fever. I thought, oh no, not again, but then I heard these words. "I'm here". Kristin was lying at the top of my bed; I was at the bottom so I could watch her. After God spoke those words, the thought came to me what would you do if she didn't have the fever. I pulled her down where I was, and we started to play. By the time her dad came home around 3:00, she was completely healed. (Glory). The Great Physician had spoken – "I'm here"… I remember that day as if it was yesterday. God stepped on the scene and bought with him benefits: healing for Kristin's body and peace for my troubled mind. (Gal 3:13-14). This time she received her healing without the need for medication. God healed her.

There's absolutely nothing like when God speaks or shows up in your situation. My God, My God… The scriptures say not to forget his benefits. (Psalms 103:2)… When God shows up, you can rest and go to bed. It's a done deal. He handles the night shift. He showed up that morning and gave us a miracle (supernatural healing), for which I was truly thankful.

The SuperNatural: Generational Anointing:

I'm amazed at the generational anointing on my family's lives also. They also experience the supernatural moves of God in their day-to-day lives. I thank God for the family he has placed me in because it's not unusual to get a call, God showed me this, or I saw this in a vision, or I dreamed this about you. It's awesome to watch the Spirit of God move in family members.

Below are a few examples of generational anointing, starting with my daughter Kristin:

Kristin (Daughter) *– David was scheduled for surgery. Kristin was just a little girl, but I'd taught her the word of God. I told her, let's pray. She said "okay mommy." She went first. I thought she'll lay hands on him and pray; then I'll really pray afterward. She walked up to him and laid her small baby hands on him, and the words that came out of her mouth were that of a seasoned warrior (the Holy Spirit himself spoke). She was too young to know those words. I stood with my mouth open when she finished; all I could say was "Amen". Why mess up what the Holy Spirit had to say. His recovery was astounding. He went back to work after two months. A guy he worked with asked him, "What are you doing here? He'd had the same surgery and was off six months. He said my wife and daughter prayed for me. God is awesome.*

Kristin *– A friend of Kristin and his family moved out of town. She hadn't heard from him in years. She came into my room that morning and said she dreamed her friend had moved back and was standing at her locker. When she came home that day, she was so excited. The very same young man she'd dreamed about was suddenly standing over her at her locker as she was getting her books out for her next class. They'd move back to Indy. God is awesome.*

Nancy (Sister) *– God told Nancy about the SuperNatural power that would produce creative miracles. This is what He said: People would come out of wheelchairs without being touched, like Peter and his shadow. That we would do mighty works, new limbs, and things like that. (Hallelujah, Praise the Lord) Same as my dream about the woman coming out of the wheelchair while I was preaching (Awesome). Nancy said that in her dream, what she* *heard and saw was – What use to be the supernatural (in the creative order) will become the natural – Also, in the dream, our family was praising God for the manifestation of the supernatural. (See: Kenneth Hagin 1980 Prophecy)*

Cathy (Aunt), Rosa (Aunt), Rena:

Cathy had the open visions concerning members of our family. It was Rosa, and my job to pray until what she saw was changed in the spirit if it wasn't in line with the will of God. – On earth, as it was in heaven. I was so drained when it was over. One thing I was assigned, I couldn't get it changed until I prayed in the spirit (tongues). I've never experienced that before. It was so draining, but I can see the benefits of those prayers today.

We live in a day where it appears that wrong is right and right is wrong. People are persecuted for their faith. But I encourage you to press on anyway because in the end, when the final forces of good versus evil, good will triumph. Jesus' defeat of Satan must be enforced because Satan is an outlaw. He doesn't abide by the rules (the Word of God). Luke 9:1-2.

God has promised SuperNatural assistance to ensure our victory against evil forces. The ability to communicate with the Father will determine your victory or defeat. I encourage you to find that place where your heart and the heart of God are one. It's a place of rest, a place of peace, and a place of power - it's a place where miracles happen. The SuperNatural is a place where you can watch the impossible become possible - watch defeat turn into victory - watch God at his best working all things together for man's good and his glory... Amen

The SuperNatural: The Prophet

There have been countless times in my life when I've been in trouble or in need that God stopped by to see about me. Whether to correct me, teach me, or just to say "I love you", it is an awesome experience. His presence can be overwhelming. When he first started training me, there was so much correction that I almost didn't want to hear his voice. I remember one day, I was expecting him to correct me because it had been a while. I waited for him to say something. He said, "You've grown up." I was happy and surprised to hear those words.

Not that I have attained everything, but I no longer required daily corrections as before. We can't be fully used in the Kingdom until we mature in the things of God. I admonish you to grow up, don't be like me. (Heb 5:12-14) Grow up so that God can use you in the office (Apostle, Prophet, Evangelist, Pastor, and Teacher), He has called you. For those who are not called the 5-fold ministry, there is still so much to do in the Kingdom. We need you, and we need each other.

The Office of Prophet

I operate under the anointing of the Prophet. It has its challenges, but God placed Prophets in the church to speak to his people. The Priest goes to God, representing the people. The Prophet goes to the people representing God. Some prophets are called to the Nations, while others are called to local assemblies. When God wants to do new things, He reveals them to the prophet, and it's the prophet's assignment to relay the message to the people. It's not his/her job to convince the people to accept the word. While the word is being spoken, The Holy Spirit will impart that message within the spirit/heart of men. The message can be informative or a warning; either should be taken seriously. The condition of the heart determines whether or not a man will receive the word. (Amos 3:7) I write the prophetic word given; later, I go back to check the validity of that word. We need to test and prove all things like the scriptures state.

Prophets should know their realm of authority. In most cases, their sphere of influence is not universal; that's why two prophets can be saying opposite things. In one place, God may be telling a church it's time to sow, and in another place, He can say it's reaping time. Not every prophetic word is for you. Not every prophet is called to speak into your life. Watch his/her words and see if they align themselves with the word God has placed in your heart. Watch his accuracy to see if he is on target with what God is speaking to your heart. I don't argue with people on words The Father has given me because "Time Will Tell." (1 Thess 5:21, Eccl 3:1) We all miss it at times, so don't throw out the messenger (the Prophet) with the message. Ask God where you missed it. (Mat 17;19). Spending more quality time with God is most important if you want to get back on the right track.

The SuperNatural: Angelic Beings

In these last days, God is using the SuperNatural to change natural (carnal) things of this world through acts of the Holy Spirit. Angels are on assignments to come to our aid and defense. Our hearts must be in tune with the Holy Spirit to discern what spirit is operating at any given time. We have as an arsenal of weapons to fight against the strategies of the enemy: God (The Father, The Son, and The Holy Spirit), The Word of God, and Angels. We stand secure in the grace of God, knowing that we have a covenant right to the blessings of God and all the benefits of Calvary through Jesus Christ our Lord and Savior. God has already made provisions for us, and we receive them by faith. (Matt 18:10, Matt 6:8. Heb 4:15-16, Rom 8:26)

Rena: *My car stopped, and this man appeared out of nowhere and fixed the problem. It was a temporary fix, but he told me exactly what to tell the car dealer. As I wrote what he was saying, I turned to say "Thanks," and he was gone. He had disappeared.*

Demonic Angels:

The weapons of our warfare are not carnal, but they are mighty through God to the pulling down of strongholds. (2 Cor 10:4-6) Many people don't believe there is a demonic world. They are real regardless of personal opinion. There are others who maximize their existence. They think everything is demonic. Some things we do are just the unregenerate flesh which can be influenced by demonic entities. Demons are real, but we overcome them by the blood of the Lamb and the word of our testimony. Recently God spoke to my spirit, Supernatural Breakthroughs, via angelic help. We sure could use their help because what we're up against these days are assignments straight from hell.

We live in a time where the SuperNatural move of God is desperately needed but greatly scorned and ridiculed. The demonic world is depicted as beautiful and splendid. It's treated as harmless and portrayed as innocent. But take it from someone who knows, it's not harmless, it's not innocent. We glorify death, vampires, evil, and the dark side through games, book series, movies, and other trinkets of Satan. I'm amazed at how nudity is glamorized in the way some celebrities dress during family-hour where our children are exposed to their ungodly lifestyles. (Rom 1:28-32)

Satan wants to find an avenue to enter our lives, wreak havoc and cause death and destruction. Souls are at stake, and we must be watchmen on the wall and not asleep on our post. God does not change, nor does His standard of living, and in the final analysis of all things, He will judge the world and its inhabitants according to His Word, not what's politically correct. (2 Cor 5:10)

Angelic Duties:

Created Beings that served the Creator and his Creation

Are obedient to God - 2/3 of the Heavenly Host

Bring messages from God - Gabriel

Can't preach the gospel, but they can take you to someone who can

Comfort and minister to Believers (Heirs of God)

Execute God's Judgment – Can be provoked

Give Praise and Worship to God (Sing)

Hearken to the voice of the Word of God

Have great power, although they are not omnipotent (all-powerful) like God

Move quickly (faster than light) through the atmosphere

Possess intelligence, but they are not omniscient (all-knowing) like God

They have rank and names (Good=Angels) (Bad=Fallen Angels and Demons)

War in both the heavenly and earthly realms for the King, His Kingdom, and His Heirs (although they are not omnipresent) like God

Angels are our reinforcements to carry out the plan, strategies, and assignments of God

Work against Satan (Kingdom of Darkness) and with the God (The Kingdom of Light)

Assist man in carrying out their God-given assignments

Fallen Angels: Satan and Demons - They were disobedient to God - 1/3 of the Angels

Everyone has at least two angels from birth— Mat 18:10

People never become angels (Sons) — Angels never become people (Servants)

Angels and People of the Bible:

Abraham - Gen 22:11

Adam & Eve - Gen 3:24

Assyrians - 2Kings 19:35

Balaam - Num 22:31

Cornelius - Acts 10:3

Daniel - Dan 10:12-13

David - 2 Sam 24:17

Disobedient Angels - Heb 2:2

Elijah - 2Ki 2:11

Elisha - 2Ki 6:13-17

Gad - 1Chron 21:18

Gideon - Judge 6:12-13

Hagar - Gen 21:17

Hebrew Boys - Dan 3:25-26

Herod - Acts 12:23

Hezekiah - Isa 37:15,36

Joseph - Matt 1:19-20

Joshua - Zec 3:16

Joshua the High Priest - Zec 3:1

Lazarus: The Beggar - Luke 16:22

Lot - Gen 19:15

Manoah and Wife - Jdg 13:2-3, 21-22

Mary and Joseph - Luke 1:26-27, 1:30

Moses - Acts 7:35

Nathanael - John 1:51

Nebuchadnezzar - Dan 3:28

Paul - Acts 27:23

Peter - Acts 11:13

Peter and the Apostle - Acts 5:19

Phillip - Acts 8:26

Shepherd - Luke 2:10, 13

Trouble the Waters - John 5:4

The SuperNatural: The Place I Meet God (Elohim)

Israel - Ex 14:19	*Unsaved - Matt 25:41*
Jacob - Gen 31:11	*Uzziah - Isa 6:1-2*
Jesus - Matt 4:11, Matt 25:31	*Women at Jesus's Tomb - Luke 24:5, 23:55*
John - Rev 1:1	*Zacharias and Elisabeth – Luke 1:18-19*

The SuperNatural: End-Time Events

My prophetic friends seem to be locked in a battle about end-time events. On one side, it's all light, and on the other side, it's all darkness. I stand in the middle because the scripture says; it was light in Goshen (church) and dark in Egypt (the world). Even in darkness, God will have a remnant of light so that people can come to him. We must let our light so shine that men will see our good works and glorify the Father, which is in heaven.

End Time Events: *God will use whomever he chooses in the end-time: those with a heart to hear and do his purpose will be chosen. Many are chosen in the fires of life. Below are a few examples of what the Spirit of God revealed to me about the end-time. He said he was bringing some up and moving some down. Great men and women passed on to be with the Lord. It was still hard nonetheless to see them go, but their spirits and teachings live on in us today.*

Batons and mantels have been passed on - now is the time to pick up our mantels, our weapons and run with what we've been taught with the aid of the Holy Spirit. In this (what is believed), the last move of God there will be: Shifting occurs, and Mantels are passed. Below are my journal entries of what God has spoken to me and others concerning these occurrences.

Journal Entries

Prophetic Shifting:

The Shift in the Spirit

God woke me up at about 4:30 in the morning; He said the following: "There's been a shift in the Spirit. Then He said, get up and write: There's been a shift in the Spirit. Those things that used to seem impossible are now possible. It's for everyone who will reach out and grab it. (Amen).

There's been a shift in the Spirit, saith the Lord. It's time in your life for miracles, signs, and wonders because; There's been a shift in the Spirit. I've seen your faithfulness - through your praise and worship. Continue to be faithful to give and receive, but most important, to make time to worship me. I'm ready to do a new and great and mighty thing in your midst. There's been a shift in the Spirit. Lo, I'm here - Summon me, and I'll be there. There's been a shift in the Spirit. Watch me work - No Fear - No Worry - No Doubt - No Enemy can stop this because,

There's been a shift in the Spirit, saith the Lord.

New Generals:

Last year God told me about the shift. I saw the shift in my spirit again. It was like this:

There was a big connection. Everything was fitting together. Then there was a separation-the top from the bottom. The bottom shifted to the right, and it joined another top, and it fitted just perfectly. (New Generals, New Breed) It was awesome to see. - 09/30/01

The Hour Glass:

I saw an Hour Glass shifting to the right, and the people at the top were now at the bottom and vice-a-versa - 11/12

The Picture Shift:

I saw the picture; it tilted/shifted a quarter, not like the hourglass that shifted completely upside-down. - 3/14

Mantels Being Passed:

Kenneth Hagin:

I'd seen a brown bronze-ish casket at the beginning of this year (5/03).

I heard the Lord say, "There's been a shift. I'm bringing some down and moving some up".

Rev. Kenneth Hagin was hospitalized on 09/13/03 – The day I found out about it, I was so depressed, tears ran down my face, and I didn't know why. I went to the internet, and there was a story that he'd died, but he hadn't. Once I found out that he was in the hospital, the burden lifted instantly. I felt that someone in his family was still holding on to him. He died on 09/19/03. I've felt this way about the passing of family members before, but this was a new experience. My interpretation: Our souls were knitted together in ministry.

The Mantel: I saw a gold baton. A couple of days later, I watch the memorial services for Brother Hagin. His son had a gold baton in his hand to pass on to those who would carry on his father's legacy.

Paul Crouch:

Dream: Jesus (in a white robe) was standing in the sky but also standing close to us. I was so excited about it. Nancy had the same experience, but she was a little concerned about it. I explained to her not to be afraid that he was here to protect and fellowship with us. Something was going on, but I didn't know what it was. At about 1:10, Jentzen Franklin posted on Facebook that Paul Crouch had passed (11/30). The last time He'd died three times but was brought back. This time he didn't make it. – 11/30/14

John Paul Jackson:

Dream Vision: I kept having dreams of going to new locations. Then I had a vision of a new location and a huge new house under construction. I knew something was up in the spirit realm, but it wasn't adding up. I posted it on FB 02/18/15 at 12:44 in the prophecy group. That day at about 3:04, I found out that John Paul Jackson had passed. New Location, New House - 02/18/15

Mantels have been passed. Many great leaders had fought a good fight, and now a crown of righteousness was laid up for them. Now we must take what we have learned and use them as weapons to enforce the enemy's defeat and bring the Word of the Gospel to the lost. Flowing in the anointing of the SuperNatural will become Natural to the Born-again Believer as we find that place in God where we are adorned with his presence, hear his voice, and act on his Word. Be very careful of accepting the mantel that's passed down to you.

There has been much controversy about the Faith message versus the Grace message. But the truth of it all is one without the other produces an imbalance in the Body of Christ.

I carry the Mantles of my mentors. I walk in the prophetic, which includes dreams, vision, tongues, interpretations of dreams, and tongues (on some occasions).

Dream: I see a Wonder Woman crown. (4/03/16)

I went to the web to look her up to see what's going on because it's not a real royal crown. Wonder Woman has a crown with 1-star in the middle. I hadn't remembered that. I wrote the dream, and then I shared it with my friends. A few weeks later, Texas, the Lone-Star state, has a devastatingly massive flood. Sometimes when I have problems interpreting a dream or vision, I do these things: 1) Ask the Holy Spirit for the revelation 2) Pray in the Spirit 3) I look up dream symbols in my Dream Dictionary 4) I write the Interpretation 5) I watch and review for accuracy.

THE SUPERNATURAL: THE PLACE I MEET GOD

The SuperNatural: The Place I Meet God (Elohim)

When man is one with the Creator in the realm of the SuperNatural, God reveals his secrets, the secrets of the universe - Miracles, Signs, and Wonders happen. Get Ready... Be Ready... We have been called to live in the SuperNatural power and presence of God - for the Good of man and Glory of God – Amen.

I have studied with some great men and women over the years. Some I just stand in awe of their gifting. I have titles from Teacher–Apostle. But I would give them all up for the anointing of God to destroy yokes and burdens the people of the earth are facing. (Acts 10:38) God doesn't use titles when he addresses me; He calls me Rea and Rena when I'm in trouble. What a mighty and wonderful God we serve.

Lessons Learned:

In the last days, God is using the SuperNatural to change the natural, and things will be accelerated because we are in the last days, and Christians are up against a formidable enemy

We will receive divine assistance in these last days. There be more for us than against us

We receive all the benefits of Calvary through knowing the love and peace of God, prayer, and praise because He has already made provisions for us through his Word

Prophets should know their region of authority - Every word of a prophet may not be a word for you, therefore prove all things, and hold fast that which is good

Expect Creative Miracles

Listen for the voice of the Lord because He's speaking words of life

It's dark and getting darker in the world, but Jesus is the light, and his light is getting lighter and brighter in the kingdom.

Prophetic Words:

The Supernatural is a special place where miracles happen. It's the place where prayers are answered, and dreams are fulfilled. It's the realm where God and man are one and nothing; absolutely nothing is impossible. The SuperNatural is the place I/we meet God.

CHAPTER SEVEN

PROPHECY: THE SUPERNATURAL MOVE OF GOD

Scripture:

1 Cor 13:9-10 - For we know in part, and we prophesy in part.

10 But when that which is perfect is come, then that which is in part shall be done away.

Prophecy is the SuperNatural move of God – when God and Man are one. God's thoughts become our thoughts. His words become our words, and we move accordingly.

Story: Lines in the Sand - The Prophetic

I watched my prophetic friends draw lines in the sand about the outcome of a current situation – opposite opinions - opposing views. Both sides are so sure that they're right. Some so arrogant it's almost scary. How dare you challenge me. I've heard from God, I've heard him for years, and now you come along and think you're someone. I'm right, and you're wrong. I've learned not to argue prophetic words. State your case and move on. **Time (God) Will Tell…**

Satan wants to divide and conquer. When prophets become disagreeable, they play into the hands of Satan. It is at that point they lose their focus. They become distracted. They become more concerned about their reputation (past victories) than the current word or move of God. They are now open to Satanic attacks (light vs. darkness — lies vs. truth). As a young Christian, I remember God telling me never to go to my word to prove that you're right; go to my word to find Truth. (I could be wrong). That was a lesson many prophets of today had to learn the hard way.

People suffer when the prophetic is off, and we miss it. The world and Satan want to pervert the things of God. That's where the word wicked comes from — it means twisted. When the prophetic is off, we major in minor things (distracted) and minor in the major things of God (delusion). Examine every prophetic word in light of the Word and moving of the Spirit of God.

As a note to the wise, watch giving prophetic words when you become too emotionally involved in the situation. You must stay in a place to hear God whether you like the word given or not. What is God saying - What direction is he moving, must be our major focus, not our opinion or reputation. You must evaluate the words that you hear, to see if it aligns with the things/thoughts of God for this time, this season and for God's purpose.

Jonah is a perfect example of a prophet who was too emotionally involved in the assignment God had given him. Let's examine the outcome.

The Story of the Prophet Jonah

Jonah 3:1-5, 9-10 - And the word of the Lord came unto Jonah the second time, saying,

2 Arise, go unto Nineveh, that great city, and preach unto it the preaching that I bid thee.

3 So Jonah arose, and went unto Nineveh, according to the word of the Lord. Now Nineveh was an exceeding great city of three days' journey.

4 And Jonah began to enter into the city a day's journey, and he cried, and said, Yet forty days, and Nineveh shall be overthrown.

5 So the people of Nineveh believed God, and proclaimed a fast, and put on sackcloth, from the greatest of them even to the least of them.

9 Who can tell if God will turn and repent, and turn away from his fierce anger, that we perish not?

10 And God saw their works, that they turned from their evil way; and God repented of the evil, that he had said that he would do unto them; and he did it not.

Jonah 4:1 - But it displeased Jonah exceedingly, and he was very angry.

Don't be like Jonah. Judgment is the last alternative for God (warning before destruction). Upon receiving the message from Jonah, Nineveh repented, God forgave them and didn't destroy the nation. Because Jonah had experienced negative encounters with the Ninevites, he wanted to see them destroyed. Be very careful; your enemy may not be God's enemy. God will judge this world by His word and not the dictates of mere men. Being able to hear the voice of God and flow in the Spirit is crucial/critical.

In contrast to the actions of Jonah lets, let's look at The Prophet Samuel.

The Story of the Prophet Samuel

1 Sam 16:1, 6-7 …fill thine horn with oil, and go, I will send thee to Jesse the Bethlehemite: for I have provided me a king among his sons.

6 And it came to pass, when they were come, that he looked on Eliab, and said, Surely the Lord's anointed is before him.

7 But the Lord said unto Samuel, Look not on his countenance, or on the height of his stature; because I have refused him: for the Lord seeth not as man seeth; for man looketh on the outward appearance, but the Lord looketh on the heart.

The prophecy was right (God), but the interpretation was wrong (Samuel). Samuel had part of the prophecy, which meant he had to continue to listen to God to see what he would say. David was the chosen vessel, not Eliab or his other brothers who were in the house with his father. David wasn't even a consideration to be anointed as the new King of Israel. If Samuel had gone by sight and emotions, he would have missed God. When God moves we move. When prophets fail to realize they only have part of the prophecy, they fail to continue their walk with God receiving new and fresh revelations. Getting part and not the full prophecy is what we call a miss.

How to recover from a missed prophecy:

- Don't try to minimize it
- Repent for missing the prophecy
  Admit that you missed it (Humility)
  Spend time with God and see where you've missed it
- Don't make excuses for your actions
- Place the situation and your reputation under the blood of Jesus
- Receive forgiveness
- Keep it moving, now from your corrected place

We must humble ourselves and own up to a missed word. 1 Cor 13:9 - For we know in part, and we prophesy in part. —Learn from the missed prophecy - Get up - Dust yourself off - Keep it moving.

Be careful when you mock the men and women of God who have missed certain prophecies. This doesn't make them false prophets. Your labels mean nothing to God. God doesn't make judgments according to your mislabeling of the prophet or the prophecy. If the man or woman of God has asked forgiveness for a missed prophecy or sin and God has forgiven him, you may find yourself on the wrong side of judgment.

Saul is a perfect example of how your actions can alter the course of a given prophecy.

Saul the Disobedient King

Divine Instruction

1 Sam 15:1-3 - Samuel also said unto Saul, The Lord sent me to anoint thee to be king over his people, over Israel: now therefore hearken thou unto the voice of the words of the Lord.

2 Thus saith the Lord of hosts, I remember that which Amalek did to Israel, how he laid wait for him in the way, when he came up from Egypt.

3 Now go and smite Amalek, and utterly destroy all that they have, and spare them not; but slay both man and woman, infant and suckling, ox and sheep, camel and ass.

Saul's Disobedience

1 Sam 15:9-11 - But Saul and the people spared Agag, and the best of the sheep, and of the oxen, and of the fatlings, and the lambs, and all that was good, and would not utterly destroy them: but everything that was vile and refuse, that they destroyed utterly.

10 Then came the word of the Lord unto Samuel, saying,

11 It repenteth me that I have set up Saul to be king: for he is turned back from following me, and hath not performed my commandments. And it grieved Samuel, and he cried unto the Lord all night.

Saul Lost of Rulership

*1 Sam 16: 1 - And the Lord said unto Samuel, **How long wilt thou mourn for Saul, seeing I have rejected him from reigning over Israel?** Some promises of God or conditional while others aren't.*

Saul's rulership was predicated on his obedience. God is looking for men and women who will remain humble and obedient as they rule and reign over His people and the preaching of His word and will. Watch that the love of power and things do not supersede the love for God and his people. God first, people second. In that order only. When we put God and his word first, he will align the necessary people as he sees fit. Sir John Dalberg-Acton wrote: Power tends to corrupt, and absolute power corrupts absolutely.

Disobedience and Rebellion is sin.

1Sam 15:3 - For rebellion is as the sin of witchcraft, and stubbornness is as iniquity and idolatry. Because thou hast rejected the word of the Lord, he hath also rejected thee from being king.

By the way, that was not the first time Saul had been disobedient to the word of God. 1 Sam 15:22 - And Samuel said, Hath the Lord as great delight in burnt offerings and sacrifices, as in obeying the voice of the Lord? Behold, to obey is better than sacrifice, and to hearken than the fat of rams. God chooses what he will receive as a sacrifice. Many people want to give God what's left or what they want to give him. Sorry to say, it won't work. He wants obedience as he describes it. Nothing less.

False Prophets

Even worst than those in leadership being disobedient is when the people have to deal with false prophets. These men and women don't speak for God. Their primary purpose is usually is to rule over people, line their pockets with their money, and prevent the truth from being told. A lying and murderous spirit is often-times attached to them. They rule, commanding the people (their subjects) to total obedience to their every word, whether they are right or wrong.

There is always the question of whether or not there are false prophets. Let's examine it now.

Question: Are there false prophets. Of course, there are false prophets (teachers, witnesses, christs, apostles, brethren, accusers). They're found in both the new and old testament.

Everything God created, Satan has twisted and perverted to establish his kingdom. I caution you to be aware. Examine everything in line with the Word and Spirit of God. I strongly suggest that you don't make your determination that a man is a false prophet on one incident. Examine everything in line with the Word and with the aid of the Holy Spirit. If all you know about the Word is what you have heard someone say or preach, how can you truly examine a prophet's word.

The Bible admonishes us to do the following:

2 Tim 2:15 - 15 Study to shew thyself approved unto God, a workman that needeth not to be ashamed, rightly dividing the word of truth.

1 John 4:1-3 - Beloved, believe not every spirit, but try the spirits whether they are of God: because many false prophets are gone out into the world.

2 Hereby know ye the Spirit of God: Every spirit that confesseth that Jesus Christ is come in the flesh is of God:

3 And every spirit that confesseth not that Jesus Christ is come in the flesh is not of God: and this is that spirit of antichrist, whereof ye have heard that it should come; and even now already is it in the world.

Prophecy is one armor in the arsenal of God against the wiles and strategies of the Devil and the lack of knowledge of man in any given situation. The bible says not to despise prophesying.

1 Thess 5:20-21 - Despise not prophesyings. Prove all things; hold fast that which is good. You have the right to question any prophecy given to you.

We need everything in God's arsenal to fight an adversary that is arrayed against us 24/7. If we can't hear or won't hear God through the voice of the Holy Spirit, we are in serious trouble. We have great power at the mention of the name of Jesus: When I pray, I thank God for the Covenant Speaking Blood of the Lord Jesus Christ. I have a covenant of protection and provision with God against the workings of Satan. Armed with God's word for any situation, we begin to walk in the SuperNatural power and flow of God. (Hallelujah, Glory to God)

*2 Cor 10:4-6 - (For the weapons of our warfare are not carnal, but mighty through God to the pulling down of strong holds;) Casting down imaginations, and every high thing that exalteth itself against the knowledge of God, and bringing into captivity every thought to the obedience of Christ; And having in a readiness to revenge all disobedience, **when your obedience is fulfilled.***

The prophets are given words from God to instruct the people (prophecy). We must trust God with all our heart and lean not to our own understanding, and he will lead us into victory after victory. God knows the end from the beginning. He knows the past, the present, and the future.

He can look at all spectrums of life in one moment and give that information to a natural man with SuperNatural anointing - for the good of man and the glory of the father. One Word From God can change people, places, things, ideas, and concepts.

Now back to my friends… My prophetic friends missed it because they were more concerned about the man and the things he'd done in the past; they neglected and ignored what he was doing now (aligning himself with ungodly men). As a result, they missed it. God gave me a word concerning some of the things going on - If God has made you a promise, you don't have to sin to get or keep it. The prophets didn't spend enough objective time with God to get the heart of God on that current situation. People now label them as false prophets, and the world maligned and mocked God's supernatural things.

As I've said for years, the Christian life was never designed to be lived without the leadership and guidance of the Holy Spirit. He is the one that comes alongside and takes hold together with us against our infirmities - Our inability to produce desired results. What we don't know, remember God does. The Holy Spirit knows everything about everything. He's waiting for your invitation to enter your circumstances. Just Ask Him.

Prayers of an obedient and righteous man avail much. When we are walking with God in the Spirit, in Jesus' name, we have access to legions of angels just at the mention of that Name. There is an anointing that breaks chains and destroys yokes when we are one with God. We are not alone - God is teaching our hands to war and our fingers to fight. He has given us authority over Devils (demons) Luke 9:1-2. Use whatever weapon the Holy Ghost reveals in every battle. Hear and Obey.

Always remember our battle is not with people, especially those of the household of faith. Primarily, Preachers speak on behalf of the people to God, but the Prophet speaks on behalf of God to the people) People and even Nature itself waits for the Sons of God to manifest their God-given rights in the earth to bring order to chaos. Rom 8:19 - For the earnest expectation of the creature waiteth for the manifestation of the sons of God. The prophetic and spoken word does this.

Yes, even the earth waits for the manifestation of the sons of God. For the heirs of God to take their rightful place in the earth. We can't do that effectively without a Word from God (the prophetic). As children of God, we must: See– What God Sees, Hear-What God is saying, Love as God loves, Command as God commands (occupy until he comes), Rule and Reign, We are the ones to speak to darkness-light, chaos-order, evil–good, sickness-health, life-death, poverty-wealth, defeat-victory, unrighteousness-righteousness, lies-truth. In Christ, we are the difference-makers in the earth. God working with us and confirming His Word with signs following.

Luke 9:1-2 - Then he called his twelve disciples together, and gave them power and authority over all devils, and to cure diseases. 2 And he sent them to preach the kingdom of God, and to heal the sick.

Mark 16:17-18 - And these signs shall follow them that believe; In my name shall they cast out devils; they shall speak with new tongues;

18. They shall take up serpents; and if they drink any deadly thing, it shall not hurt them; they shall lay hands on the sick, and they shall recover.

God has revealed the role of the Prophet and Prophetic in the scripture.

The Prophet in Scripture

Amos 3:7 - Surely the Lord God will do nothing, but he revealeth his secret unto his servants the prophets.

Eph 4:11-13 - And he gave some, apostles; and some, prophets; and some, evangelists; and some, pastors and teachers;

12 For the perfecting of the saints, for the work of the ministry, for the edifying of the body of Christ:

13 Till we all come in the unity of the faith, and of the knowledge of the Son of God, unto a perfect man, unto the measure of the stature of the fulness of Christ.

These offices, gifts will exist until Jesus comes back to the earth. They work in unity of faith and knowledge unto a mature man. If God works in unity, what happens when we operate in division? It is no longer God working but Satan, who is described in 2 Cor 4:4, as the god of this world. When the prophet is on point, lives are changed for the good of man and the glory of God.

The prophets or prophetic community must also realize they are not lone rangers in the things of God. We, too, are subject to other prophets. Working together works – use it whenever possible. Stop putting your faith in anything or anyone but God – He is our source; everything else is a resource.

1 Cor 14:29-32 - Let the prophets speak two or three, and let the other judge.

30 If anything be revealed to another that sitteth by, let the first hold his peace.

31 For ye may all prophesy one by one, that all may learn, and all may be comforted.

32 And the spirits of the prophets are subject to the prophets.

Personal Prophecy Given

My best friend (Vivian Ingram) came with a not-so-good doctor's report. She said, "Rena, my doctor has been running tests, and there's something wrong with my blood. They're not sure, but they think I have leukemia. Please ask God what's wrong with me". I told her I will, and if he tells me, I'll tell you. Knowing that whatever I told her is the direction she would take. I admit I struggled with it. It's not like you will get a new job or something like that prophecy.

This is a matter of life and death.

That night as I prayed, I asked God, and when he said, she's iron deficient. I waited for more, but that's all he said. When I spoke with her, I told her what I believed God had said. We waited for the test results from her last blood draw. Her doctor informed her that they were going to start her on an iron pill regiment, and that was it. I'd heard right… Thank you, Jesus.

Summary:

The prophetic is a vital part of the success against the onslaught of demonic forces arrayed against God's children – known and unknown. If the prophetic and prophets weren't necessary for the Body of Christ, God would not have placed them in the Body. We must use every means God has provided for us to ensure complete and lasting victories. This gift can be used for the good of man when it is given and controlled by the Holy Spirit.

This gift can also be used against us when it is twisted and perverted by Satan or even prophets in the wrong timing of God. Walking in humility and the timing of God is extremely important. Examine everything in the light of God's Word, regardless of who gives the word. The prophetic is an added benefit in our everyday walk. It brings clarity and insight into situations after situations in our lives. When we don't know, know that God does and is willing to help us, and prophecy is one of the avenues he uses. Embrace it. Walk-in it.

Moving in the prophetic is an awesome and humbling experience. It goes beyond your intelligence and ignorance. It's earth defying to truly hear and know the mind and heart of God - God the creator of the universe. It defies human logic that God would speak and reason with man his creation. When the natural meets the SuperNatural - Where time and space are no longer a part of the equation – It is the place where miracles happen.

Lessons Learned:

Do not argue prophetic words. State your case and move on. **Time (God) Will Tell***.*

Never go to my word to prove that you're right. Go to my word to find Truth (you could be wrong).

When the prophetic is off, we major in minor things (distracted) and minor in the major things of God (delusion).

Watch giving prophetic words when you become too emotionally involved in the situation.

If you miss it, you're not necessarily a false prophet.

We must humble ourselves and own up to missing a prophecy

Learn from it (Repent (Humility) - Get up - Dust yourself off - Keep it moving.

Because Saul became more concerned about what the people said than God - God rejected him.

Stop putting your faith in anything or anyone but God – He is our source; everything else is a resource

My prophetic friends missed it because they were more concerned about the man and the things he'd done in the past; they neglected and ignored what he was doing now.

THE SUPERNATURAL: THE PLACE I MEET GOD
Prophecy: The SuperNatural Move of God

We need everything in God's arsenal to fight an adversary that is arrayed against us 24/7. If we can't hear or won't hear God through the voice of the Holy Spirit, we are in serious trouble.

Prophetic Words:

The prophetic is a vital part of the success against the onslaught of demonic forces arrayed against us, but the battle is the Lord's. Victory is assured because of the finished work of the cross of Calvary.

"When you move in the spirit, God and man are one. Go for it in my name and watch me work - Trust Me"...Saith the Lord.

One word from God can change the outcome of any battle.

CHAPTER EIGHT

BIBLICAL RESTORATION

Scripture:

Joel 2:25 - <u>And I will restore to you the years</u> that the locust hath eaten, the cankerworm, and the caterpillar, and the palmerworm, my great army which I sent among you.

Leviticus 6:4-5 - Then it shall be, because he hath <u>sinned</u>, and is guilty, that he shall restore that which he <u>took violently</u> away, or the thing which he hath <u>deceitfully gotten</u>, or that which was <u>delivered him to keep</u>, or the <u>lost thing which he found,</u>

5 Or all that about which he hath <u>sworn falsely (lies)</u>; he shall even restore it in <u>the principal, and shall add the fifth part more thereto, a</u>nd give it unto him to whom it appertaineth, in the day of his trespass offering. (Principal = 100, 1/5 = 20, Total 120%)

Story:

Sitting in my favorite chair, I asked God what the coming year would bring. Quickly I heard one word, <u>"Restoration"</u>. I waited to see if there was anything else, but nothing else, no explanation, no nothing. That's it... That's all...

Minutes later, Kristin walks into the room and shares her dream with me.

The Dream: There are three buses: Kristin is on one, and her Father is on another. She gets off the bus to go inside the building to get the other people because they are about to leave. As she goes inside, all three buses take off. She's annoyed because her dad let them leave without her. She calls him on his cell and says, "Come back and get me!" The bus he's on turns around and comes back to get them.

Interpretation: Restoration will begin when you declare it. "Come back and get me!" The Father represents God. The bus is the path she is taking. The permissive will of God happens when we are on another path, but the perfect will of God is when we are on the same path with him.

What a great God, He is. Sometimes in life, when things aren't going the way we would like or desire, when things are out of control, we must use our God-given authority to change them and bring them back into order. When we cry out to our Heavenly Father, he sends help and delivers us. When the bus came back, Kristin and her Father are now on the same bus, the same path. Notice: Nothing happened until she spoke the words, "Come back and get me"… (Mark 6:47-51)

Still amazed and thinking about the revelation of "Restoration", later that morning, I got up to read my Facebook messages, and lo and behold, Joseph Prince theme for the year was "The Year of His Restoration". That was the confirmation I needed. As time passed, I wondered what would be restored and how. I knew I had to start speaking the word God had given me, make my stand to bring my purpose into existence: "RESTORATION," and I needed to do that now!!! (Matt 18:16)

Over the last several months, I felt I was in a never-ending storm. One thing happened after the other. Being out of work and all the pressures that come with unemployment and bill payment is in of itself a lot to deal with, but on top of that, I faced several personal crises, one after the other. If it had not been for the Lord on our side, I know we would not have made it.

Personal Challenges:

April	*Death: Barb (Mentor1 and my best friend) passed*
September	*Death: Kristin's Grandmother (Her Father's Mom) passed*
November	*Death: Myles Monroe (Kingdom Teacher) passed*
December	*Death: My mom (Mentor2) passed*
January	*Hospitalization: Kristin's Father was hospitalized*
	False Accusation: I was accused of a devastating family matter that was later proven to be untrue
February	*Death: John Paul Jackson (Mentor3) passed*
March	*Hospitalization: Kristin's God-son was hospitalized*
April	*Death: Kristin's cousin was killed*
	Death Certificate Delay: We were still waiting for my Mom's death certificate. A 10-day process had taken 117 days
May	*Restoration: Finally, we saw God begin to bring restoration and closure (order) in our lives*
	In a dream, my mom tells Kristin, "I heard you've been looking for me."
	It was then; she started to let go of some of the pain and grief she'd been carrying.

Spending time with God throughout all these ordeals was the best thing for me. After seeing Him fix somethings I had no control over (situations I had to give over to Him and let him work it out), I began to hear his voice clearer. Again "The Book" came up in my spirit. I just couldn't wrap my mind around being able to write a book on my own. I felt too weak to change, but I was miserable where I was. Something had to give. What would I say that others hadn't already said and better? It had been years since he told me to write a book giving short reminders along the way, but I didn't think I could, so I didn't. I hadn't surrendered, so I was in disobedience. God never gives you an assignment that he doesn't factor himself into the equation. I needed to trust Him. I needed to surrender.

One morning while thinking about surrendering to the will of God about everything in my life, including the "The Book", Kristin walks in. As I'm telling her about critiquing and typing my aunt's papers, Kristin says," You've helped others write their books; when are you going to write your own?" That was it!!! It was time to be obedient to God and start writing. So I decided to put it all in God's Hand as I called for Restoration of the things I'd recently lost. At that point, I saw God begin my restoration when I let go of me and embraced Him for the outcome of all the things I was facing, including The Book.

Restoration (Leadership Shift):

With every shift in the spirit, God brings restoration. Change is always needed to bring things back into order, back into alignment. Over the last couple of years, God has been telling me more and more about the Shift in the Spirit of Leadership. I saw great leaders go home to be with the Father. In my own personal life, most of the mentors who had been instrumental in my growth as a person and as a Minister of the Gospel have gone to be with the Lord. Two things they taught me that I want to pass on was on the subject of Character and Testing:

Character: *A person can truly be anointed, but their character can be very questionable. It's dangerous to operate in an anointing with open sin and rebellion in your heart because you open yourself to destruction and familiar spirits. (**Lev 19:31, 1 Sam 28:7, Num 22:4-6**)*

Testing: *Another ministerial lesson learned, all who will be used of God must be able to stand in a crowd or alone on the other side of the mountain with absolutely no one during certain seasons of testing. Testing builds character, slowly and painfully. (James 1:3-4) During this season, I felt isolated, and sometimes I wondered if it had been worth it all. Often-times I felt alone with the prophetic word God had given me because I wasn't aligned with the things others were saying. I stayed the course, knowing that "Time Will Tell" what was right and what was wrong.*

After going through rejection and isolation, God began to speak Restoration into my life/spirit. Little things at first, but gradually they got bigger. Things I've been waiting and fighting for years were changing on my behalf. It was a great feeling. God never leaves you without His love or His word. During this season of my life, He told me every day he loved me, and he continues to reassure me of His love. Where there are injustice and loss, there must come restoration to bring about wholeness.

The devil is an equal opportunity strategic troublemaker, but God is greater, and he can restore to us all that the enemy has taken from us and add punitive damages. (Praise the Lord). One of the things Pastor Prince taught about Restoration was that when God restores, he does it with greater quantity or quality. When man restores, it's usually not the same in value and rarely, if ever of greater value. (Job 1-42)

Restoration (Quantity and Quality)

Here are a few biblical restoration scriptures that illustrate both quantity and quality: God knew the time would come when we would need to recover from losses that occurred in our past (1Sa 30:8), whether the loss was our doing or the doings of others. Praise God he has a plan for our recovery even before we ask, but we are instructed to ask. (Mat 7:11)

Restoration Quantity:

Here are some Old Testament scriptures representing restoration levels. If the New Testament is established on better promises, at least you can start here:

Leviticus 6:4-5 (100% + 20%) - Then it shall be, because he hath sinned, and is guilty, that he shall restore that which he took violently away, or the thing which he hath deceitfully gotten, or that which was delivered him to keep, or the lost thing which he found, Or all that about which he hath sworn falsely; he shall even restore it in the principal and shall add the fifth part more thereto, and give it unto him to whom it appertaineth, in the day of his trespass offering.

Job 42:10 (2X) - And the Lord turned the captivity of Job, when he prayed for his friends: also the Lord gave Job twice as much as he had before.

Ex 22:1 (4X-5X) - If a man shall steal an ox, or a sheep, and kill it, or sell it; he shall restore five oxen for an ox, and four sheep for a sheep.

Proverbs 6:31 (7X) - But if he (Thief) be found, he shall restore <u>sevenfold;</u> he shall <u>give all the substance of his house</u>.

God has made provisions for your recovery from loss; these may range from 120% or 2-7 times what was lost. Expect to recover all plus punitive damages. Restore, Restore, Restore.

Restoration of Years:

Even if years go by and you haven't seen the fulfillment of your promise, that's okay; you are in good company. Many of the Patriots of old had to wait years for the fulfillment of their God-given promise: David (15-Kingship), Joseph (13-Palace), Abraham (25-Isaac),

Moses (40-Leadership), Jesus (30-Ministry), Paul (3- Sabbatical). Keep looking because your day will come. God is faithful.

Joel 2:25 (Years that the enemy has stolen from you) - <u>And I will restore to you the years that</u> the locust hath eaten, the cankerworm, and the caterpillar, and the palmerworm, my great army which I sent among you.

2 Kings 8:2 - And the woman arose, and did after the saying of the man of God: and she went with her household, and sojourned in the land of the Philistines <u>seven years.</u>

2 Kings 8:5-6 - And it came to pass, as he was telling the king how he had restored a dead body to life, that, behold, the woman, whose son he had restored to life, <u>cried to the king</u> for her house and for her land. And Gehazi said, My lord, O king, this is the woman, and this is her son, whom Elisha restored to life. 6 And when the king asked the woman, she told him. So the king appointed unto her a certain officer, saying, <u>Restore all that was hers, and all the fruits of the field since the day that she left the land, even until now.</u>

Quality:

Not everything taken from you can be replaced in quantity. For example, the death of a love-one. God will replace that loss with quality. Example: You can't have seven husbands, at least not at one time. (Mat 22:25-26) Expect to recover all as the woman above and King David did when he lost his wives and children (1Sam 30:8, 18). – Recover All

Psalms 23:3 (Mind, Will, and Emotion) *- He restoreth my soul: he leadeth me in the paths of righteousness for his name's sake.*

Man like God is triune… He is Spirit, Soul, and Body. For man to be whole and at peace, every aspect of his life must be whole. Life can hit you so hard that your soul begins to doubt God, man, and yourself. It's important in troubled times to anchor our soul with hope in God and God alone because everything else is shakable, and he is our rock, fortress, and foundation. Perhaps this saying says it best, "Never forget in the dark what God showed you in the light."

Psalms 51:12 - (Joy - Strength) *- Restore unto me the joy of thy salvation; and uphold me with thy free spirit.*

The joy of the Lord is our strength. When we're down-n-out (depressed), it takes its toll on us and our ability to stand against the wiles and tricks of the enemy. When we have the strength of God, we can run through troops and leap over walls (Ps 18:29). It's not by our own might that we stand, it's by God's strength and ability along with his love, grace, and faithfulness. (Zec. 4:6)

Isaiah 42:22 (Restore when it is proclaimed) *- But this is a people robbed and spoiled; they are all of them snared in holes, and they are hid in prison houses: they are for a prey, and none delivereth; for a spoil, and none saith, Restore.*

In order for restoration to begin in our lives, we must begin proclaiming it. The blessings of God are typically not automatic but are obtainable through the avenue of the spoken word. Just say it - Say it until you see it. (120% Restoration…) Proclaiming the problem is not the way out. Decree a thing and keep silent if you can't say something positive. Ask the Father to show you what he sees. Watch your words, Repent when you become negative, and Move on without Condemnation. Train yourself to stop using negative words.

Examples: Dying to go. My feet are killing me. I'm catching a cold. I was so mad that I couldn't see straight. I can't do that to save my life. It cost an arm and a leg. Love you to death. Your words establish you so - Speak Life.

Watch your words, for they are what is building/defining your future. Say what God says and nothing else. "One word from God can change anything or anybody at any time and anywhere."

***Isaiah 58:12 – (Desolate places)** - And they that shall be of thee shall build the old waste places: thou shalt raise up the foundations of many generations; and thou shalt be called, The repairer of the breach, <u>The restorer of paths to dwell in.</u>*

God will restore things that have long been lost and deserted, even when men say it can't be done. If God has given his word, he is faithful, and he can walk into your past and fix things humanly impossible to fix. He stands outside of time and orchestrates our lives. He's that kind of God knowing the end from the beginning. He's already decreed good for our lives; we need to come into agreement with him.

***Jeremiah 30:17 – (Health)** - <u>For I will restore health unto thee, and I will heal thee of thy wounds (chronic condition)</u>, saith the Lord; because they called thee an Outcast, saying, This is Zion, whom no man seeketh after.*

Healing is provided for our Body because of God's love and the finished work of the Cross of Calvary (Jesus). Even in the Old Testament, God provided a way of escape from the curse of sickness (Numbers 21:9).

In some cases, restoration can be both quality and quantity. I call this recover all. Generational restorations occur on this level of blessings. Many enemy attacks are generational, and the cycle must be broken according to the covenant we have in Christ Jesus (Gal 3:13, Heb 8:6). Let's examine a few scriptures to confirm this.

Quality and Quantity:

Luke 4:18-19 (Everything) - *The Spirit of the Lord is upon me, because he hath anointed me <u>to preach the gospel to the poor</u>; he hath sent me <u>to heal the brokenhearted</u>, to preach <u>deliverance to the captives</u>, and recovering of <u>sight to the blind</u>, to set at liberty them that are <u>bruised</u>, 19 <u>To preach the acceptable year of the Lord (Jubilee)</u>.*

Lev 25:10-11 - *And ye shall hallow the fiftieth year, and proclaim liberty throughout all the land unto all the inhabitants thereof: it shall be a jubilee unto you; and ye shall <u>return every man unto his possession,</u> and ye shall <u>return every man unto his family</u>. A jubilee shall that fiftieth year be unto you: <u>ye shall not sow, neither reap</u> that which groweth of itself in it, nor gather the grapes in it of thy vine undressed.*

The Year of Lord (Jubilee) occurred every fiftieth year. When the trumpet sounded on the Day of Atonement, liberty was proclaimed throughout the land. All properties taken for unpaid debts would have to be returned to the original owners. Jewish slaves were set free to go back to their families. It was also a time of reaping Harvest blessings: a time to begin again and recover all. This was an Old Testament blessing, but Jesus is our Jubilee our New Testament blessing.

Ruth 1:3-5 (Personal Loss): *And Elimelech Naomi's husband died; and she was left, and her two sons. And they took them wives of the women of Moab; the name of the one was Orpah, and the name of the other Ruth: and they* *dwelled there about ten years. And Mahlon and Chilion died also both of them; and the woman was left of her two sons and her husband.*

Ruth 4:13 (Restoration) - *So Boaz took Ruth, and she was his wife: and when he went in unto her, the Lord gave her conception, and she bare a son.*

Ruth (Moab) and Naomi (Jewish) lost everything. Ruth returned to Israel with Naomi (her mother-in-law). There she would recover all. She married Boaz (Kinsmen Redeemer), one of the richest men of that area, and they had a son named Obed. Obed begat Jesse, and Jesse begat King David. What a restoration… We need to declare our blessings and recover all from our past losses, especially generational losses – Recover all.

Declaration of the Blessing

God has already ordained good things for his children, but there's an enemy that has set himself arrayed against us. We, like our Father, must declare what he has already spoken to us through his word. His word will not return void. However, if we don't declare God's word of restoration, chances are we won't be seeing it in our lives or the lives of others. When we declare God's word, not only are we blessed, but those around us are also blessed. When men see the goodness of God, they turn to him. (Rom 2:4 …the goodness of God leadeth thee to repentance). Yes, they will see your good works and glorify God. Restoration begins and flourishes when Hope is alive with an earnest expectation of good. Speak it, Declare it, Decree it, Seize it.

Declaration: *I declare everything lost be restored 120% (Lev. 6:4-5) - I declare RESTORATION over my life because Christ has redeemed me from the curse, and now I stand under the blessings of the Lord to recover all. RESTORATION" has begun in my life – today, In Jesus Name… Thank you, Father Amen.*

Lessons Learned:

Restoration has already been decreed in Heaven; we need to come into agreement (alignment) with that word by speaking it: declaring and decreeing it.

"One word from God can change anything or anybody at any time and anywhere."

Note: Many will question, if you're so anointed, why do you experience these attacks of the devil? My answer is if Satan tested Jesus, who was without sin, surely you can expect him to try, tempt, and test you.

Prophetic Words:

Restoration shall be in quantity or quality... Declare it now...

I declare and decree 120% Restoration for every loss as a Jubilee unto my family and me from God the Father and the Lord Jesus Christ and made known through the work of the Holy Spirit- Amen

CHAPTER NINE

RESTORATION OF THE CHURCH

Restoration of the Church:

At the beginning of the year, God gave me the word "Restoration", but my thoughts were so limited to my own personal situation, I'd missed the big picture until I heard a message from Bishop Michael Pitts on the subject of Jubilee. God is going to restore the church, the five-fold ministry, and his people, basically, so we can bring revival to the church and an awakening to the world. Afterward, he will come and take us out of here. There will be light in the church and darkness in the world. Christ is not coming back for a defeated church, for his word says, the gates of hell shall not prevail against the church. He is equipping the church with spiritual weapons: Kingdom keys and principles to bring in the last Harvest of Souls. (Matt 16:15-19)

Always remember God is our first line of defense against all that is evil and the evil one.

Restoration of all things must be accomplished before Jesus returns. (Acts 3:20-21) This world's system is corrupt and failing. The only stability we have is in Christ and Him alone. Many of the children of God have died, suffered great loss and persecution. Our victory is not the product of our own personal accomplishments or abilities; it is in the rest and obedience of man and the grace of God that unites heaven and earth to give us decisive win, victory after victory. (Prov 13:22)

96

Acts 3:20-21 - And he shall send Jesus Christ, which before was preached unto you: 21 Whom the heaven must receive until the times of restitution of all things, which God hath spoken by the mouth of all his holy prophets since the world began.

Only when we know and exercise the following can we obtain the victory that comes from the very throne room of Grace:

1) *Know the love of God for his children*
2) *Know our authority in the finished work of the Cross (via the Word of God)*
3) *Begin to pray in the Spirit to obtain the perfect will and purpose of God for any given situation*
4) *Begin to speak to mountains (Grace, Grace - Restore). There is a word from God for any given situation.*

In the darkness of this world, we are to speak light to dispel the darkness. According to scripture, the elements of creation will adhere to the voice of the Word of the Lord (Psalms 103:20, Mat 17:20). Creation itself waits for the manifestation of the Sons of God to take their rightful place and declare and decree restoration. (Rom 8:19-22)

Anything that stole your harvest, dreams, visions, plans, and purposes must be restored because, as you know, you can't give what you don't have. The earth was put under bondage when man sinned. Jesus came to place things back under the control and authority of the born-again man. Although Christ is in heaven, we are not helpless to fend for ourselves. Before leaving the earth, he prayed for the church and left instructions to the disciples to stay until the empowerment of the Holy Spirit came upon them. On the day of Pentecost, that was accomplished. (Acts 2:1-4, Gal 4:6)

The church has, for the most part, entertained doctrines of men rather than the unadulterated Word of the Living God (Jehovah). As man continues to fall and, in many cases, reach rock bottom, he will prayerfully look again unto Jehovah God, the one who delivers and sets men free. The world and creation itself are waiting for the Sons of God to manifest the Spirit of God on the earth, in power and authority against the wiles of the Devil and the deceitfulness of mortal men. It shall be accomplished. Time is being accelerated, and the anointing is being increased. (Matt 4:4, Luke 9:1-2)

Luke 10:19 *- Behold, I give unto you power to tread on serpents and scorpions, and over all the power of the enemy: and nothing shall by any means hurt you*

God will not be defeated, not even in this hour in which we live. There shall be a Restoration of Family, Peace (Nothing Missing, Nothing Broken, Nothing Shattered), Finances, Joy, Strength, Marriage, Children, Your Name (Honor), New Beginning, and Restoration of Your Edge (Confidence) per Dr. Medina Pullings. The purpose and will of God will be accomplished, and the manifestation of his presence will be evident in those who boldly stand and proclaim his Word and Message among the heathen and the church at large. Creative miracles and the abundance of blessings will give beauty for ashes in the lives of the Children of God. Blessed to be a Blessing. (Isa 61:3, John 14:27)

People will come into the Kingdom for such a time as this, and God's house shall be full. His glory will be manifested, and His love will be on display in the hearts and actions of his children. Many of the lost will come to a saving knowledge of Jesus Christ as Savior and Lord. Many will be healed and delivered from the powers of darkness. For the earth shall be filled with the knowledge of the glory of the Lord, as the waters cover the sea. (Hab 2:14) Then the "End" shall come. Come Lord Jesus, Come. (Matt 5:18, Matt 24:14)

Two other ways God is restoring the church are:

- *Prayer – John 14:14 - If ye shall ask anything in my name, I will do it.*
- *Impartation of Divine Favor (Great Grace) – Acts 4:33 - And with great power gave the apostles witness of the resurrection of the Lord Jesus: and great grace was upon them all.*

Prayer

Prayer is a vitally important way God is restoring the church. Prayer lines have been given the mandate to pray and speak into the atmosphere the prophetic word of God. I'm currently participating on several online ministries prayer lines (Hollywood FBC, Serenity, Harvest Issachar, Call Unto Me, and many others). I'm amazed at the zeal of power, prayer, and praise that goes out over these lines. Prayer warriors are uniting together for the good of man and the glory of God. It's awesome.

Prayerlessness can lead to ultimate defeat in the course of life for the born-again believer. Prayer is an essential part of the daily Christian life. Prayer is how we predominately communicate with God. It's a time when we get to share our deepest thoughts, greatest concerns and just spend time with the Father: Sometimes just to tell him it hurts right here. We are invited on a daily basis to come and talk with Him - Come, let us reason together saith the Lord. Always remember Prayer changes things.

Men and women of the Bible developed a special relationship with God that bought about many awesome answers to prayer. Prayer is talking to God, and God talking to man. After the fall of Adam, communication between God and man was severely damaged, but Jesus came to restore our relationship. The gift of speech places man in a category or class to communicate with the Father like no other creature.

Gen 2:7 - And the Lord God formed man of the dust of the ground, and breathed into his nostrils the breath of life; and man became a living soul.

Gen 3:9-10 - And the Lord God called unto Adam, and said unto him, Where art thou? 10 And he said, I heard thy voice in the garden, and I was afraid, because I was naked; and I hid myself.

Prayer is also a time we receive instructions from God. We hear the very heart of God as it beats with such love for his children. Many find great comfort just sitting in his presence. The warmth of his presence gives us or reassures us of his great care for us (watchfully and affectionately).

1 Peter 5:7 - Casting all your care upon him; for he careth for you.

The course and fate of many have been changed because of the special relationship and communication between God and man. Biblical examples of men and women who change their destinies and the destine of others are mentioned below:

Examples:

Moses intercedes for the children of Israel after they sin worshipping an idol – Ex (32:7-12).

Abraham intercedes for Sodom and Gomorrah on behalf of Lot - Gen 18:25-33

Jonah's life was saved when he refused to preached the gospel to the Ninevites - Jonah 1-4

David's life was spared when he impregnated Uriah's Wife - 2 Sam 12:13

Hannah prayed, and God gave her the son she desperately desired - 1 Sam 1:9-12

Jesus prayed for the men that crucified him - Luke 23:34

A Centurion prayed for his servant who was sick - Matt 8:5-10

A woman of Canaan whose daughter was grievously vexed with a devil prayed - Matt 15:22

Two Blind men wanting their eyes open cried out (prayer) - Matt 20:30-33

There were many other instances when prayer changed the course of a given situation. It is never God's desire to destroy man, but some behavior will lead to the destruction of the flesh. When you walk with God and talk with him on a daily basis, you will be surprised at what God will do just because you ask. I'm going to share a story concerning this very thing. God has not changed; he is still working miracles on our behalf. John 16:23-24

Answered Prayer: Lee's Grave Condition

The phone rings. It's my cousin Toni. She's really upset. She calls me Peewee. She said, "Peewee, Lee's in the hospital, and he's gravely ill. The doctors don't think he will last until morning. His body is shutting down." He needed a pacemaker, he was on dialysis, he was placed in a medically induced coma, and he'd been severely depressed on top of that. I later learned that he'd died twice and was resuscitated by a biker before making it to the hospital. He had so many things wrong with him; it would take a miracle. I told her I would pray.

Getting off the phone, sitting in my recliner, I began to talk to God. I told him that Lee has never really known love. His relationship with his mom had been strained, and he never really had the chance in life to be loved unconditionally. I asked God to give him another chance at life where he could be shown real love. My heart went out to him because of the warped sense of love he had developed during his rocky journey through life. He was looking for love in all the wrong places.

Despite the earlier prognosis, he made it through the night. Days later, Toni posted on her Facebook page that he had turned around for the good. She was thanking God for his life. God had given us a miracle. He left the hospital and entered into rehab, and eventually was discharged to go home. It's been almost three years now, and Toni said he's doing great. I tell you, as the songwriter penned, God is a Way Maker, Miracle Worker, and Promise Keeper. Thank you, Jesus…

We have favor with God because of His love for us, His covenant with us through the name and blood of Jesus. All these things are revealed to us through his word and the power and leading of the Holy Spirit. Oh, that we would take advantage of such a privilege, such an honor.

Impartation of Divine Favor (Great Grace)

God is also restoring his church by imparting a season of Divine Favor (Grace). We must believe that God is going to help us. He is going before us and making the crooked places straight, rough places smooth – bringing order out of chaos and snatching victory out of the very mouth of defeat by believing that God has a good plan for your life and that he will use his resources (supernatural powers) to bring it to pass.

A yielded heart to God in the moving of the Holy Ghost will result in you performing supernatural acts in a natural and corrupt world bent on destroying all that God has for you. If you want to see Miracles, Signs, and Wonders, Answers to Prayer – You're going to have to get more acquainted with the Holy Ghost. Be determined that all that God has for me, I want it. The Holy Spirit will lead you in line with the Word and Will of God.

This Season – Divine Favor – Checklist

1. *Seek 1st the Kingdom of God - Matt 6:33*
2. *Spend Time with God in the Word and in His Presence – Prov 4:20-23*
3. *Hear the Voice of God with clarity and openness of heart - Rev 2:7*
4. *Trust God (Have Faith in God) - Mark 11:22*
5. ***Obey what you are told (Led by the Holy Spirit) - 1 Sam 15:22***
6. *Embrace What God is saying in this Season - Just Do It – Ezek 36:26*
7. *Declare His word (in the face of opposition) – 2 Kings 4:26*
8. *Be patient and stay in faith until the manifestation – Heb 6:12-15*
9. *Stand in Grace, Walk by Faith, Live in the Love of God and the sweet communion of the Holy Ghost - Rom 5:2-5*
10. *Maintain an attitude of gratitude with a thankful heart (Give God the Praise – From Start to Finish) - Eph 5:20*

1) *Matt 6:33 - Seek 1st the Kingdom of God - Priority*

But seek ye first the kingdom of God, and his righteousness, and all these things shall be added unto you. Ask God for wisdom, knowledge with a hearing, and understanding heart. You will need it in this journey called life.

2) *Prov 4:20-23 – Spend Time with God in the Word and in His Presence (Building an intimate relationship with the Father- Hand vs. Heart)*

   My son, attend to my words; incline thine ear unto my sayings. 21 Let them not depart from thine eyes; keep them in the midst of thine heart. 22 For they are life unto those that find them, and health to all their flesh. 23 Keep thy heart with all diligence; for out of it are the issues of life.

3) *Rev 2:7 - Hear the Voice of God with clarity and openness of heart - Hear with an open heart*

   He that hath an ear, let him hear what the Spirit saith unto the churches; To him that overcometh will I give to eat of the tree of life, which is in the midst of the paradise of God.

4) *Mark 11:22 – Trust God (Have Faith in God) - Foundational Truth (You've got to trust God when you can't trace Him. When you have more questions than answers)*

   And Jesus answering saith unto them, Have faith in God.

5) *1 Sam 15:22 – Obey what you are told (Led by the Holy Spirit) - Hear & Do.*

   And Samuel said, Hath the Lord (as great) delight in burnt offerings and sacrifices, as in obeying the voice of the Lord? Behold, to obey is better than sacrifice, and to hearken than the fat of rams.

6) *Ezek 36:26 - Embrace What God is saying in this Season - Just Do It*

   A new heart also will I give you, and a new spirit will I put within you: and I will take away the stony heart out of your flesh, and I will give you an heart of flesh.

7) *2 Kings 4:26 – Declare His word (in the face of opposition) – Expect Opposition*

   Run now, I pray thee, to meet her, and say unto her, Is it well with thee? is it well with thy husband? is it well with the child? And she answered, It is well. – You are not a hypocrite when you say what God says about you in the face of contradictory circumstances.

8) *Heb 6:12-15 – Be patient and stay in faith until the manifestation – Delay is not Denial*

   That ye be not slothful, but followers of them who through faith and patience inherit the promises. 13 For when God made promise to Abraham, because he could swear by no greater, he sware by himself, 14 Saying, Surely blessing I will bless thee, and multiplying I will multiply thee. 15 And so, after he had patiently endured, he obtained the promise.

9) *Rom 5:2-5 - Stand in Grace, Walk by Faith, Living in the Love of God and the sweet communion of the Holy Ghost – Grace, Faith, and Love is an explosive combination that leads to victory with God and man*

   By whom also we have access by faith into this grace wherein we stand, and rejoice in hope of the glory of God. 2 Cor 5:7 - (For we walk by faith, not by sight:)

10) *Eph 5:20- Maintain an attitude of gratitude with a thankful heart (Give God the Praise – From Start to Finish)*

    Giving thanks always for all things unto God and the Father in the name of our Lord Jesus Christ;

In Summary:

*Pray (Speak) – **Listen (Hear)** – Obey (Do) – Praise (Hallelujah). Prayer is about you – Praise is about God.*

The Place of Praise originates in the heart and can be manifested in any and every place. The Holy Spirit is to us (the Church) as God was to Adam – Jesus was to His Disciples.

We are students of the Holy Spirit (to be taught and led by Him). Embrace Him – He has the gifts Jesus died that we might have. He has power. He gives authority. He is the Spirit of Truth – He is the Paraclete – He Is here to help us obtain the blessings and maintain our relationship with God through our Lord and Savior Jesus Christ finished work. He is our: Advocate - Comforter – Counselor – Helper - Intercessor – Standby – Strengthener – Teacher.

Don't allow the traditions of men, denominations, well or mean-spirited people stop you from embracing the Holy Spirit and all He has to offer the Body of Christ (fruit and gifts). Many lives, including your own are at stake. Go into all the world and preach the gospel. Without the anointing of the Holy Spirit, our preached words are of little effect. However, those with the anointing turned the world upside down. - John 20:22 - And when he had said this, he breathed on them, and saith unto them, Receive ye the Holy Ghost:

Mark 16:20 - And they went forth, and preached everywhere, the Lord working with them, and confirming the word with signs following. Amen.

If what you're doing is manifesting miracles, signs, wonders, and souls being saved, then, by all means, continue what you're doing. If not, and you want to see change, please consider what I've mentioned throughout this book. The more we yield to the prompting of the Holy Spirit, the more of a victorious life we'll live being blessed and a blessing – for the good of man and glory of God. Amen

Lessons Learned:

God is our first line of defense against all that is evil and the evil one.

God is going to restore the church, the five-fold ministry, and his people, basically, so we can bring revival to the church and an awakening to the world.

Prayerlessness can lead to ultimate defeat in the course of life for the born-again believer.

*Pray (Speak) – **Listen (Hear)** – Obey (Do) - Praise (Hallelujah).*

Prayer is about you – Praise is about God.

Prayer changes things…

Prophetic Words:

A yielded heart to God in the moving of the Holy Ghost will result in you performing supernatural acts in a natural and corrupt world bent on destroying all that God has for you.

If you want to see Miracles, Signs, and Wonders, Answers to Prayer – You're going to have to get more acquainted with the Holy Ghost. The Holy Spirit will lead you in line with the Word and Will of God.

CHAPTER TEN

DAUGHTERS OF ZION (THE DREAM)

Scripture:

Zech 2:10 - Sing and rejoice, O daughter of Zion: for, lo, I come, and I will dwell in the midst of thee, saith the Lord.

Story:

Being rejected by my denomination because I was a woman, I wanted to give other women a platform to speak outside of the confines of the four walls of tradition and religion. As a result, I felt led to form an organization where we could embrace other women in their pursuits to use their God-given abilities. We would go beyond all denominational lines and embrace any and all women who had a heart for God. As a result, Daughters of Zion was formed in 2003. It would be an organization to wake and stir up the gifting in individuals and promote unity in the Body of Christ and community. Working with the IRS to obtain my 501(3) C was the first article of business. Minister Donna Branham's faithfulness will always be appreciated in this assignment.

Others helped to fulfill the dream and desires in my heart. In November of 1997, I was ordained by the late Bishop Ronnie L. Roundtree. When it wasn't popular to ordain women, he stepped out of the norm and ordained women called by God. For that, I shall always be grateful. There were others instrumental in the success of Daughters of Zion. My best friends in the ministry: Malvern (Mel) and Barbara (Barb) Neville, were the first to accept my calling, and their support was so greatly needed and appreciated. God brought Barb into my life in 1979. He wanted me to attend Sunday school, but I didn't. They both were Sunday school teachers.

As a child, I loved going to Sunday school, but as time passed, I stopped going; but because I wanted my daughter to experience the same joy, I decided to finally give in (it was more than worth it). There is nothing like the Word of God, especially in times of trouble. Many churches have stopped having Sunday school classes, but I believe it's important to study the word with no hidden agenda, just the unadulterated word of God in a fuller content with class participation. Just because you teach the word doesn't mean people have gotten it. Q&A is vitally important for both the teacher and the student.

Barb was not only a Sunday School Teacher, but she was the Sunday School Superintendent. I watched her faithfulness and her love for the word of God. It so changed my life. She and Mel prayed with and for me long hours as I started my journey into ministry. They were such blessings. We became more like family than friends and co-workers. Sister Ora Bailey, Evangelist Elizabeth Shepherd Porter (ESPRM), and Pastor Johnnie Mae Edmonds were all very instrumental in my walk as I finally surrendered to attending Sunday School and teaching classes at church.

My mentor and great friend Bishop J. Laverne Tyson's faith in me was extremely important in my pursuit to walk in the things of God. He allowed me on several occasions to speak on his radio program. He always put me at ease on his show. The late Evangelist Jada West and I appeared on the TV show Religion in the News with host Theresa Weatherby and on the Amos Brown Show concerning our ministries' events. Bishop Mary L. Guthrie, with her busy schedule, was kind enough to attend our conferences. It was such an encouragement to me personally when she walked through the door and helped minister to the women.

My uncle and aunt, Pastor Leroy and Co-Pastor Florida Lawrence (Shining Star MBC), and their congregation supported our ministry in donations, work, and memberships. We couldn't have made it without them. Countless others freely gave their services to make DOZ conferences a success. Finally, last but not least, my family's love and support were a solid foundation for our conference success. I could always count on them to be there and do whatever we needed to be done.

Daughters of Zion (DOZ) conferences would serve as a platform to hear and give a Word from the Lord. The first years were such a struggle, but the conference results made it worth it. One year while trying to decide which theme to use, my daughter woke up out of a sound sleep and said, "Thanks mommy", turned over, and went back to sleep. It confirmed the theme we would use that year "We Give (God) Thanks"- A Testimony of Thankfulness (Psalms 100:1-5).

We found a hotel that the women seemed to enjoy. It was a great site with great food! The prayer breakfast gave the women time to fellowship and get to know one another. I didn't want anyone coming to the conference without getting to know at least one other person. We went beyond the natural into the supernatural, the very presence of God in our worship. I watched our worship leader Melissa Peck (I call her Missy) move from being a worship leader to accepting her calling as a Minister of the Gospel. It was so wonderful and beautiful to see! She and her husband, Pastor Errick Peck, were so faithful to attend.

At the end of each year, I would sit before the Lord to get the next year's theme. I prayed and fasted. The greatest part of the conference was God would meet us there. There wasn't ever a conference where the Spirit of the Lord didn't move. I remember there were times when I woke up, and it was like the Spirit said, come on, let's go. The conference would be so anointed that even though I was exhausted afterward, I couldn't sleep because my spirit was still going. I would just lie there because I was too tired to move physically but to awake to sleep. God would always change the flow from what was on our paper, but we didn't care. We just moved with the flow in the spirit. I can feel it even now as I'm typing.

Remembering one year, God instructed me to ask Apostle Wanda Studdard, and I argued with him because she had her own TV program; she and her husband had a church and a radio program. I thought she would be too busy even to consider it. So I didn't call her. God didn't change his mind, and neither did I. Finally, I gave in, just to satisfy Him. Still thinking that she would say, "No" and then I could move on to get someone else, I picked up the phone, called her office, and left a message asking her to call me. When she called, I was shocked. She was so nice and said she would love to do it. I was almost speechless. Thinking back now, when has God ever been wrong? When Apostle Studdard came, she bought the women of her church in full force, and needless to say, that was a great conference.

One thing that really startled me was the fact that the less I did in these conferences, the more God did. One year I decided not to have a conference. I waited until the last minute, and so there wasn't time for all the up-front preparation. My thing was, God, if you want me to do this, it's on you, and that conference was by far the greatest conference we'd ever had. I was amazed. What was happening here? It was simply; He wanted to be more involved in everything, from start to finish.

I thought all my praying, fasting, worshipping, and everything else I did were the things I needed to do to have God move in the conference. It's a lot easier if you just ask Him what He wants. Those things are great, don't get me wrong, but then it's what you've done, not what He's done. It didn't take me long; I changed my methods, I did less, and He did more, and we were all blessed. Sometimes God's enthusiasm and excitement reminded me of a kid who wanted to go outside and play. He would be in my bedroom when I woke up, He would be at the hotel when we got there, He would be there when people left, and He would be in my room when I got back home (full circle).

God knitted us together with people who had a heart for him, and when asked to do something, no matter how large or small, they would do it. Our program included praise dancing (God's Company Dance) and drama (Vision on High Production) plays as well. My friend Prophetess Nina Reed was a great blessing as she prayed for the speakers. One less thing I had to do. My family pitched in, which made everything easier. Even our children were involved. My daughter (Kristin) and the Twins (Briana and Cody Jones) would run the registration table and anything else we asked. I could always count on them. Other women discovered and began using their gifts and callings.

After every conference, there was a time to pray for individuals, and we added communion to go along with our service. We were able to plant offerings and seed into other organizations in our community, to feed and serve the homeless, and we were also able to donate to individuals in need. I thank God for the donors who gave to sponsor women who couldn't afford to pay their registration fees. We tried to assist anyone wanting to attend our conferences. I tried to get the women to eliminate the breakfast so we wouldn't have to charge a registration fee, but they weren't hearing that.

My fondest memory was of the conference on Domestic Abuse. It was there I learned and experienced some phenomenal things. While speaking on Religion in the News, as I was sitting in the back with some other people, I mentioned the theme, this girl out of nowhere said, "I was raped three times and that she hadn't ever shared it with anyone." Her friends all looked shocked. Now her healing could begin. Secrecy is what keeps many men and women in bondage. That's wasn't the only incident; there were many occurrences just like that. I learned that even in my own family, things of this nature had occurred.

On the day of the conference, God forgot our agenda and did a great work in the women there. I was amazed by their stories. One woman told how after her father passed, she went to his gravesite, stood over him, and said, "I forgive you." Other women shared their stories; I stood in amazement at the pain they'd gone through and their walk to wholeness through forgiveness. There were tears of healing and deliverance, and compassion throughout the room.

My heart and passion are for the unity of the Body of Christ as Christ is the center and object of our attention and affection. There is a special place in God where we who are natural meet the supernatural presence of God, and we are transformed into the very image of His likeness, which I call worship. Worship is the place where God comes down, and we go up and where we meet and are one. My calling and these conferences are designed to serve as a gateway to this very experience. Finally, these conferences were designed to awaken the gifting in us and unite us with other worshippers to create a harmony that can only emanate from the very Throne Room of Grace. (Heb 1:1-4)

THE SUPERNATURAL: THE PLACE I MEET GOD

Daughters of Zion (The Dream)

Lessons Learned:

True worship is not about your gifting but your heart. The place where I am one with God.

There is a special place in God where we who are natural meet the supernatural presence of God, and we are transformed into the very image of His likeness: A place of worship. I call worship the place where God comes down, and we go up and where we meet and are one.

Prophetic Word:

Sometimes less is more than enough when we are one with God (less of me, more of Him).

CHAPTER ELEVEN

CONCLUSION

Invitation to Salvation:

If you haven't personally accepted Jesus Christ as your Lord and Savior, I now invite you to ask Him into your life (heart). He loves you and is waiting to save you and make you a part of the family of God. Come, Come, Come Now – Tomorrow might be too late.

John 3:16-17 – For God so loved the world, that he gave his only begotten Son, that whosoever believeth in him should not perish, but have everlasting life. 17 For God sent not his Son into the world to condemn the world; but that the world through him might be saved.

Eph 2:8-9 - For by grace are ye saved through faith; and that not of yourselves: it is the gift of God: 9 Not of works, lest any man should boast.

Rom 10:9-10 - That if thou shalt confess with thy mouth the Lord Jesus, and shalt believe in thine heart that God hath raised him from the dead, thou shalt be saved. 10 For with the heart man believeth unto righteousness; and with the mouth confession is made unto salvation.

Acts 2:38-39 – Then Peter said unto them, Repent, and be baptized every one of you in the name of Jesus Christ for the remission of sins, and ye shall receive the gift of the Holy Ghost. 39 For the promise is unto you, and to your children, and to all that are afar off, even as many as the Lord our God shall call.

Salvation Prayer:

Father God, I come to you a sinner and ask you to forgive me of all my sins and cleanse me from all unrighteousness by the blood of Jesus. I confess with my mouth that Jesus is Lord, I believe in my heart that you have raised him from the dead, and according to your word, I am saved. Thank you, Father, that I am now the righteousness of God in Christ Jesus, and I will rule and reign in life by your Son and my Savior, Christ Jesus. Thank you, Father, for all the benefits and gifts you have given to me, and I now embrace them through the aid of the Holy Spirit. I now confess that I am Yours, and You are mine. I love you, Father God. Thank you for saving me. In Jesus Name, Amen

Gifting: Benefits of Salvation

Every good and perfect gift comes from God, so embrace them, but remember that a man's character will determine the quality of his life and the life of those who surround him.

Gal 5:22-23 - But the fruit of the Spirit is love, joy, peace, longsuffering, gentleness, goodness, faith, 23 Meekness, temperance: against such there is no law.

James 1:17 - Every good gift and every perfect gift is from above, and cometh down from the Father of lights, with whom is no variableness, neither shadow of turning.

1 Cor 12:8-11 - For to one is given by the Spirit the word of wisdom; to another the word of knowledge by the same Spirit; 9 To another faith by the same Spirit; to another the gifts of healing by the same Spirit; 10 To another the working of miracles; to another prophecy; to another discerning of spirits; to another divers kinds of tongues; to another the interpretation of tongues:

11 But all these worketh that one and the selfsame Spirit, dividing to every man severally as he will.

2 Cor 9:8 - And God is able to make all grace abound toward you; that ye, always having all sufficiency in all things, may abound to every good work:

Prayer of Blessing:

Father God, I ask that you bless the reader of this prayer.

May they experience renewed hope and faith in a God that is able to do exceeding abundantly above all they ask, think, or imagine.

May they know the love of God and the sweet communion of the Holy Ghost.

May they know they are the righteousness of God in Christ Jesus forever.

May they rule and reign in this life through your son Jesus Christ.

May they walk in their redemptive right according to Gal 3:13, Isaiah 53:4-5, and Num 6:24-26.

May they lack no good thing (Psalms 23, Psalms 91), In Jesus Name.

Father bless them, keep them, protect them, make your face shine upon them, be gracious unto them, lift up your countenance upon them, and give them your peace. Peace that passeth all understanding.

Grace be with them, mercy, and peace, from God the Father, and from the Lord Jesus Christ, the Son of the Father, in truth and love. Amen

REFERENCE

SCRIPTURES

CHAPTER ONE

THE POWER OF DEATH AND LIFE

1 John 5:14-15 - And this is the confidence that we have in him, that, if we ask any thing according to his will, he heareth us:15 And if we know that he hear us, whatsoever we ask, we know that we have the petitions that we desired of him.

1 Peter 2:24 - Who his own self bare our sins in his own body on the tree, that we, being dead to sins, should live unto righteousness: by whose stripes ye were healed.

2 Thess 1:3-4 We ought always to thank God for you, brothers, and rightly so, because your faith is growing more and more, and the love every one of you has for each other is increasing. NIV

2 Tim 1:7 - For God hath not given us the spirit of fear; but of power, and of love, and of a sound mind.

Col 2:15 - And having spoiled principalities and powers, he made a shew of them openly, triumphing over them in it.

Heb 11:1 - Now faith is the substance of things hoped for, the evidence of things not seen.

Isa 65:24 And it shall come to pass, that before they call, I will answer; and while they are yet speaking, I will hear.

John 3:16-17 - For God so loved the world, that he gave his only begotten Son, that whosoever believeth in him should not perish, but have everlasting life. 17 For God sent not his Son into the world to condemn the world; but that the world through him might be saved.

Mark 11:22 - And Jesus answering saith unto them, Have faith in God.

Matt 6:8 ….: for your Father knoweth what things ye have need of, before ye ask him.

Matt 7:7-8 – Ask, and it shall be given you; seek, and ye shall find; knock, and it shall be opened unto you: 8 For every one that asketh receiveth; and he that seeketh findeth; and to him that knocketh it shall be opened.

Matt 18:20- For where two or three are gathered together in my name, there am I in the midst of them.

Phil 4:6 - Be careful for nothing; but in everything by prayer and supplication with thanksgiving let your requests be made known unto God.

CHAPTER TWO

HOW TO RECEIVE

1 John 3:1 - Behold, what manner of love the Father hath bestowed upon us, that we should be called the sons of God...

1 John 4:16 - And we have known and believed the love that God hath to us. God is love; and he that dwelleth in love dwelleth in God and God in him.

2 Cor 1:3-4 - Blessed be God, even the Father of our Lord Jesus Christ, the Father of mercies, and the God of all comfort; 4 Who comforteth us in all our tribulation, that we may be able to comfort them which are in any trouble, by the comfort wherewith we ourselves are comforted of God.

2 Cor 4:11 - We having the same spirit of faith, according as it is written, I believed, and therefore have I spoken; we also believe, and therefore speak;

2 Cor 4:18 - While we look not at the things which are seen, but at the things which are not seen: for the things which are seen are temporal; but the things which are not seen are eternal.

Eph 3:20 - 20 Now unto him that is able to do exceeding abundantly above all that we ask or think, according to the power that worketh in us..

Gal 3:13-14 - Christ hath redeemed us from the curse of the law, being made a curse for us: for it is written, Cursed is every one that hangeth on a tree: 14

That the blessing of Abraham might come on the Gentiles through Jesus Christ; that we might receive the promise of the Spirit through faith.

Gen 1:3 - And God said, Let there be light: and there was light.

Heb 4:12 - For the word of God is quick, and powerful, and sharper than any two-edged sword, piercing even to the dividing asunder of soul and spirit, and of the joints and marrow, and is a discerner of the thoughts and intents of the heart.

Heb 11:1 - Through faith we understand that the worlds were framed by the word of God, so that things which are seen were not made of things which do appear.

Heb 13:8 - Jesus Christ the same yesterday, and today, and forever.

Isa 59:19 - So shall they fear the name of the Lord from the west, and his glory from the rising of the sun. When the enemy shall come in like a flood, the Spirit of the Lord shall lift up a standard against him.

James 2:15-16 - If a brother or sister be naked, and destitute of daily food, 16 And one of you say unto them, Depart in peace, be ye warmed and filled; notwithstanding ye give them not those things which are needful to the body; what doth it profit?

Jer 29:11-13- For I know the thoughts that I think toward you, says the Lord, thoughts of peace and not of evil, to give you a future and a hope. 12 Then you will call upon Me and go and pray to Me, and I will listen to you. NKJV

Job 38:12 - Hast thou commanded the morning since thy days; and caused the dayspring to know his place;

Mark 4:19- And the cares of this world, and the deceitfulness of riches, and the lusts of other things entering in, choke the word, and it becometh unfruitful.

Mark 4:19 - And the cares of this world, and the deceitfulness of riches, and the lusts of other things entering in, choke the word, and it becometh unfruitful.

Mark 11:23-24 - For verily I say unto you, That whosoever shall say unto this mountain, Be thou removed, and be thou cast into the sea; and shall not doubt (diakritheé – stand condemned)in his heart, but shall believe that those things which he saith shall come to pass; he shall have whatsoever he saith. 24 Therefore I say unto you, What things soever ye desire, when ye pray, believe that ye receive them, and ye shall have them.

Mark 16:17-18 - And these signs shall follow them that believe; In my name shall they cast out devils; they shall speak with new tongues; 18 .They shall take up serpents; and if they drink any deadly thing, it shall not hurt them; they shall lay hands on the sick, and they shall recover.

Mark 16:20 - And they went forth, and preached everywhere, the Lord working with them, and confirming the word with signs following. Amen.

Matt 17:20- If ye have faith as a grain of mustard seed, ye shall say unto this mountain, Remove hence to yonder place; and it shall remove; and nothing shall be impossible unto you.

Phil 4:6-8- Be careful for nothing; but in everything by prayer and supplication with thanksgiving let your requests be made known unto God. 7 And the peace of God, which passeth all understanding, shall keep your hearts and minds through Christ Jesus. 8 Finally, brethren, whatsoever things are true, whatsoever things are honest, whatsoever things are just, whatsoever things are pure, whatsoever things are lovely, whatsoever things are of good report; if there be any virtue, and if there be any praise, think on these things.

Prov 15:23- A man hath joy by the answer of his mouth: and a word spoken in due season, how good is it!

Prov 22:1- A good name is rather to be chosen than great riches, and loving favour rather than silver and gold.

Ps 34:19- Many are the afflictions of the righteous: but the Lord delivereth him out of them all.

Rom 8:28 - And we know that all things work together for good to them that love God, to them who are the called according to his purpose.

Rom 10:17- So then faith cometh by hearing, and hearing by the word of God.

Zech 4:6 - Not by might, nor by power, but by my spirit, saith the Lord of hosts.

Dance, Mark. (2016, September 28). Pastors Are Not Quitting in Droves/ Mark Dance, Retrieved July 29, 2018, from https://pastors.lifeway.com/2016/09/28/pastors-are-not-quitting-in-droves/

CHAPTER THREE

NEW SEASON OF GRACE

1 Cor 2:9-10 - But as it is written, Eye hath not seen, nor ear heard, neither have entered into the heart of man, the things which God hath prepared for them that love him.

10 But God hath revealed them unto us by his Spirit: for the Spirit searcheth all things, yea, the deep things of God.

1 Sam 16:7 - ..for man looketh on the outward appearance, but the Lord looketh on the heart.

1 Thess 5:21- Prove all things; hold fast that which is good.

2 Chron 20:22 - And when they began to sing and to praise, the Lord set ambushments against the children of Ammon, Moab, and mount Seir, which were come against Judah; and they were smitten.

2 Cor 3:18 - But we all, with open face beholding as in a glass the glory of the Lord, are changed into the same image from glory to glory, even as by the Spirit of the Lord.

2 Cor 5:21 - For he hath made him to be sin for us, who knew no sin; that we might be made the righteousness of God in him.

2 Cor 8:9 - For ye know the grace of our Lord Jesus Christ, that, though he was rich, yet for your sakes he became poor, that ye through his poverty might be rich.

Acts 19:1-8 - And it came to pass, that, while Apollos was at Corinth, Paul having passed through the upper coasts came to Ephesus: and finding certain disciples,

2 He said unto them, Have ye received the Holy Ghost since ye believed? And they said unto him, We have not so much as heard whether there be any Holy Ghost.

3 And he said unto them, Unto what then were ye baptized? And they said, Unto John's baptism.

4 Then said Paul, John verily baptized with the baptism of repentance (metanoias), saying unto the people, that they should believe on him which should come after him, that is, on Christ Jesus.

5 When they heard this, they were baptized in the name of the Lord Jesus.

6 And when Paul had laid his hands upon them, the Holy Ghost came on them; and they spake with tongues, and prophesied.

7 And all the men were about twelve.

8 And he went into the synagogue, and spake boldly for the space of three months, disputing and persuading the things concerning the kingdom of God.

Eph 2:8-10 - For by grace are ye saved through faith; and that not of yourselves: it is the gift of God:

9 Not of works, lest any man should boast.

10 For we are his workmanship, created in Christ Jesus unto good works, which God hath before ordained that we should walk in them.

Gal 3:13-14 - Christ hath redeemed us from the curse of the law, being made a curse for us: for it is written, Cursed is every one that hangeth on a tree:

14 That the blessing of Abraham might come on the Gentiles through Jesus Christ; that we might receive the promise of the Spirit through faith.

Gal 5:22-25 - But the fruit of the Spirit is love, joy, peace, longsuffering, gentleness, goodness, faith, 23 Meekness, temperance: against such there is no law.

24 And they that are Christ's have crucified the flesh with the affections and lusts.

25 If we live in the Spirit, let us also walk in the Spirit.

Gen 3:15 - And I will put enmity between thee and the woman, and between thy seed and her seed; it shall bruise thy head, and thou shalt bruise his heel.

Heb 13:8 - Jesus Christ the same yesterday, and today, and forever.

Jas 1:17 - Every good gift and every perfect gift is from above, and cometh down from the Father of lights, with whom is no variableness, neither shadow of turning.

Jer 1:5 Before I formed thee in the belly I knew thee; and before thou camest forth out of the womb I sanctified thee, and I ordained thee a prophet unto the nations.

John 1:1-5 - In the beginning was the Word, and the Word was with God, and the Word was God.

2 The same was in the beginning with God.

3 All things were made by him; and without him was not any thing made that was made.

4 In him was life; and the life was the light of men.

5 And the light shineth in darkness; and the darkness comprehended it not.

John 1:17 - For the law was given by Moses, but grace and truth came by Jesus Christ.

John 19:30-31 - When Jesus therefore had received the vinegar, he said, It is finished: and he bowed his head, and gave up the ghost. 31 The Jews therefore, because it was the preparation, that the bodies should not remain upon the cross on the Sabbath day, (for that Sabbath day was an high day,) besought Pilate that their legs might be broken, and that they might be taken away.

32 Then came the soldiers, and brake the legs of the first, and of the other which was crucified with him

33 But when they came to Jesus, and saw that he was dead already, they brake not his legs:

34 But one of the soldiers with a spear pierced his side, and forthwith came there out blood and water.

Mal 3:6 - For I am the Lord, I change not;

Mark 4:14-20 - The sower soweth the word.

15 And these are they by the way side, where the word is sown; but when they have heard, Satan cometh immediately, and taketh away the word that was sown in their hearts.

16 And these are they likewise which are sown on stony ground; who, when they have heard the word, immediately receive it with gladness;

17 And have no root in themselves, and so endure but for a time: afterward, when affliction or persecution ariseth for the word's sake, immediately they are offended.

18 And these are they which are sown among thorns; such as hear the word,

19 And the cares of this world, and the deceitfulness of riches, and the lusts of other things entering in, choke the word, and it becometh unfruitful.

20 And these are they which are sown on good ground; such as hear the word, and receive it, and bring forth fruit, some thirtyfold, some sixty, and some an hundred.

Mark 7:13 - Making the word of God of none effect through your tradition, which ye have delivered: and many such like things do ye.

Matt 9:17 - Neither do men put new wine into old bottles: else the bottles break, and the wine runneth out, and the bottles perish: but they put new wine into new bottles, and both are preserved.

Matt 26:28- For this is my blood of the new testament, which is shed for many for the remission of sins.

Phil 1:11 - Being filled with the fruits of righteousness, which are by Jesus Christ, unto the glory and praise of God.

Phil 3:13-14 - Brethren, I count not myself to have apprehended: but this one thing I do, forgetting those things which are behind, and reaching forth unto those things which are before, 14 I press toward the mark for the prize of the high calling of God in Christ Jesus.

Prov 13:12- Hope deferred maketh the heart sick: but when the desire cometh, it is a tree of life.

Ps 8:2 - Out of the mouth of babes and sucklings hast thou ordained strength because of thine enemies, that thou mightest still the enemy and the avenger.

John 1:16 - And of his fulness have all we received, and grace for grace.

Ps 40:3 - And he hath put a new song in my mouth, even praise unto our God...

Ps 100:5 - For the Lord is good; his mercy is everlasting; and his truth endureth to all generations.

Rev 1:8 - I am Alpha and Omega, the beginning and the ending, saith the Lord, which is, and which was, and which is to come, the Almighty.

Rom 1:17 - For therein is the righteousness of God revealed from faith to faith: as it is written, The just shall live by faith.

Rom 5:17 - For if by one man's offence death reigned by one; much more they which receive abundance of grace and of the gift of righteousness shall reign in life by one, Jesus Christ.)

Rom 6:4 - Therefore we are buried with him by baptism into death: that like as Christ was raised up from the dead by the glory of the Father, even so we also should walk in newness of life.

Rom 8:1- There is therefore now no condemnation to them which are in Christ Jesus, who walk not after the flesh, but after the Spirit.

Rom 8:28 - And we know that all things work together for good to them that love God, to them who are the called according to his purpose.

Rom 8:30 - Moreover whom he did predestinate, them he also called: and whom he called, them he also justified: and whom he justified, them he also glorified.

Rom 12:2 - And be not conformed to this world: but be ye transformed by the renewing of your mind, that ye may prove what is that good, and acceptable, and perfect, will of God.

Rom 10:9-10 - That if thou shalt confess with thy mouth the Lord Jesus, and shalt believe in thine heart that God hath raised him from the dead, thou shalt be saved.

10 For with the heart man believeth unto righteousness; and with the mouth confession is made unto salvation.

CHAPTER FOUR

DREAMS AND VISIONS

Acts 2:17-18 -And it shall come to pass in the last days, saith God, I will pour out of my Spirit upon all flesh: and your sons and your daughters shall prophesy, and your young men shall see visions, and your old men shall dream dreams:

18 And on my servants and on my handmaidens I will pour out in those days of my Spirit; and they shall prophesy:

Dan 2:19 - Then was the secret revealed unto Daniel in a night vision. Then Daniel blessed the God of heaven.

Dan 11:32- And such as do wickedly against the covenant shall he corrupt by flatteries: but the people that do know their God shall be strong, and do exploits.

Gen 41:16 - And Joseph answered Pharaoh, saying, It is not in me: God shall give Pharaoh an answer of peace.

Joel 2:28-29 - And it shall come to pass afterward, that I will pour out my spirit upon all flesh; and your sons and your daughters shall prophesy, your old men shall dream dreams, your young men shall see visions: 29 And also upon the servants and upon the handmaids in those days will I pour out my spirit.

CHAPTER FIVE

SPEAK LORD

1 Cor 2:9-16- But as it is written, Eye hath not seen, nor ear heard, neither have entered into the heart of man, the things which God hath prepared for them that love him.

10 <u>But God hath revealed them unto us by his Spirit</u>: for the Spirit searcheth all things, yea, the deep things of God.

11 For what man knoweth the things of a man, save the spirit of man which is in him? even so the things of God knoweth no man, but the Spirit of God.

12 Now we have received, not the spirit of the world, but the spirit which is of God; that we might know the things that are freely given to us of God.

13 Which things also we speak, not in the words which man's wisdom teacheth, but which the Holy Ghost teacheth; comparing spiritual things with spiritual.

14 But the natural man receiveth not the things of the Spirit of God: for they are foolishness unto him: neither can he know them, because they are spiritually discerned.

15 But he that is spiritual judgeth all things, yet he himself is judged of no man.

16 For who hath known the mind of the Lord, that he may instruct him? But we have the mind of Christ.

1 Cor 5:3 - For I verily, as absent in body, but present in spirit have judged already, as though I were present, concerning him that hath so done this deed...

1 Cor 9:16 - For though I preach the gospel, I have nothing to glory of: for necessity is laid upon me; yea, woe is unto me, if I preach not the gospel!

1 Cor 9:27: But I keep under my body, and bring it into subjection: lest that by any means, when I have preached to others, I myself should be a castaway.

1 Cor 14:5 - I would that ye all spake with tongues, but rather that ye prophesied: for greater is he that prophesieth than he that speaketh with tongues, except he interpret, that the church may receive edifying.

1 Cor 14:14-15 - For if I pray in an unknown tongue, my spirit prayeth, but my understanding is unfruitful.

15 What is it then? I will pray with the spirit, and I will pray with the understanding also: I will sing with the spirit, and I will sing with the understanding also.

1 John 4:6- We are of God: he that knoweth God heareth us; he that is not of God heareth not us. Hereby know we the spirit of truth, and the spirit of error.

1 Peter 5:8-9 - Be sober, be vigilant; because your adversary the devil, as a roaring lion, walketh about, seeking whom he may devour:

9 Whom resist stedfast in the faith, knowing that the same afflictions are accomplished in your brethren that are in the world.

1 Sam 3:9-10- Therefore Eli said unto Samuel, Go, lie down: and it shall be, if he call thee, that thou shalt say, Speak, Lord; for thy servant heareth. So Samuel went and lay down in his place.

10 And the Lord came, and stood, and called as at other times, Samuel, Samuel. Then Samuel answered, Speak; for thy servant heareth.

1 Tim 1:2 - Unto Timothy, my own son in the faith: Grace, mercy, and peace, from God our Father and Jesus Christ our Lord.

2 Cor 1:20- For all the promises of God in him are yea, and in him Amen, unto the glory of God by us.

2 Cor 4:13- We having the same spirit of faith, according as it is written, I believed, and therefore have I spoken; we also believe, and therefore speak;

2 Cor 4:18 - For we look not at the things which are seen, but at the things which are not seen: for the things which are seen are temporal; but the things which are not seen are eternal.

2 Cor 10:4-5 - (For the weapons of our warfare are not carnal, but mighty through God to the pulling down of strong holds;)

5 Casting down imaginations, and every high thing that exalteth itself against the knowledge of God, and bringing into captivity every thought to the obedience of Christ;

2 John 6 - And this is love, that we walk after his commandments. This is the commandment, That, as ye have heard from the beginning, ye should walk in it.

2 Kings 3:14-15- And Elisha said, As the Lord of hosts liveth, before whom I stand, surely, were it not that I regard the presence of Jehoshaphat the king of Judah, I would not look toward thee, nor see thee

15 But now bring me a minstrel. And it came to pass, when the minstrel played, that the hand of the Lord came upon him.

2 Kings 5:26- And he said unto him, Went not mine heart with thee, when the man turned again from his chariot to meet thee?

2 Tim 2:15 - Study to shew thyself approved unto God, a workman that needeth not to be ashamed, rightly dividing the word of truth.

Acts 9:31- Then had the churches rest throughout all Judaea and Galilee and Samaria, and were edified; and walking in the fear of the Lord, and in the comfort of the Holy Ghost, were multiplied.

Col 3:15 - And let the peace of God rule in your hearts, to the which also ye are called in one body; and be ye thankful.

Col 3:16 - Let the word of Christ dwell in you richly in all wisdom; teaching and admonishing one another in psalms and hymns and spiritual songs, singing with grace in your hearts to the Lord.

Col 4:6 - Let your speech be alway with grace, seasoned with salt, that ye may know how ye ought to answer every man.

Deut 29:29 - The secret things belong unto the Lord our God: but those things which are revealed belong unto us and to our children for ever, that we may do all the words of this law.

Deut 30:19 - I call heaven and earth to record this day against you, that I have set before you life and death, blessing and cursing: therefore choose life, that both thou and thy seed may live:

Eph 5:15-17- See then that ye walk circumspectly, not as fools, but as wise,

16 Redeeming the time, because the days are evil.

17 Wherefore be ye not unwise, but understanding what the will of the Lord is.

Eph 6:13 - Wherefore take unto you the whole armour of God, that ye may be able to withstand in the evil day, and having done all, to stand.

Ezek 12:25 - For I am the Lord: I will speak, and the word that I shall speak shall come to pass; it shall be no more prolonged: for in your days…

Gal 5:1 - Stand fast therefore in the liberty wherewith Christ hath made us free, and be not entangled again with the yoke of bondage.

Gal 5:6 - For in Jesus Christ neither circumcision availeth anything, nor uncircumcision; but faith which worketh by love.

Gen 2:7- And the Lord God formed man of the dust of the ground, and breathed into his nostrils the breath of life; and man became a living soul.

Heb 4:3 - For we which have believed do enter into rest…

Heb 10:23 - Let us hold fast the profession of our faith without wavering; (for he is faithful that promised;)

Heb 12:2 - Looking unto Jesus the author and finisher of our faith; …

Isa 30:21 - And thine ears shall hear a word behind thee, saying, This is the way, walk ye in it, when ye turn to the right hand, and when ye turn to the left.

Isa 42:8 - I am the Lord: that is my name: and my glory will I not give to another, neither my praise to graven images.

Isa 55:8- For my thoughts are not your thoughts, neither are your ways my ways, saith the Lord.

James 3:2 - For in many things we offend all. If any man offend not in word, the same is a perfect man, and able also to bridle the whole body.

John 4:24 - God is a Spirit: and they that worship him must worship him in <u>spirit and in truth</u>.

John 5:39 - Search the scriptures; for in them ye think ye have eternal life: and they are they which testify of me.

John 6:63 - It is the spirit that quickeneth; the flesh profiteth nothing: the words that I (Jesus) speak unto you, they are spirit, and they are life.

John 14:26 - But the Comforter, which is the Holy Ghost, whom the Father will send in my name, he shall teach you all things, and bring all things to your remembrance, whatsoever I have said unto you.

Luke 12:11-12 - And when they bring you unto the synagogues, and unto magistrates, and powers, take ye no thought how or what thing ye shall answer, or what ye shall say:

12 For the Holy Ghost shall teach you in the same hour what ye ought to say.

Mark 11:22 - And Jesus answering saith unto them, Have faith in God.

Mark 16:17-20 - And these signs shall follow them that believe; In my name (Jesus) shall they cast out devils; they shall speak with new tongues; 18 .They shall take up serpents; and if they drink any deadly thing, it shall not hurt them; they shall lay hands on the sick, and they shall recover. 19 So then after the Lord had spoken unto them, he was received up into heaven, and sat on the right hand of God. 20 And they went forth, and preached everywhere, the Lord working with them, and confirming the word with signs following. Amen.

Matt 16:19 - And I will give unto thee the keys of the kingdom of heaven: and whatsoever thou shalt bind on earth shall be bound in heaven: and whatsoever thou shalt loose on earth shall be loosed in heaven.

Matt 17:20 - And Jesus said unto them, Because of your unbelief: for verily I say unto you, If ye have faith as a grain of mustard seed, ye shall say unto this mountain, Remove hence to yonder place; and it shall remove; and nothing shall be impossible unto you.

Prov 4:20-23 - My son, attend to my words; incline thine ear unto my sayings.

21 Let them not depart from thine eyes; keep them in the midst of thine heart.

22 For they are life unto those that find them, and health to all their flesh.

23 Keep thy heart with all diligence; for out of it are the issues of life.

Prov 20:27 - The spirit (heart) of man is the candle of the Lord, searching all the inward parts of the belly.

Ps 8:2 - Out of the mouth of babes and sucklings hast thou ordained strength because of thine enemies, that thou mightest still the enemy and the avenger.

Ps 22:3 - But thou art holy, O thou that inhabitest the praises of Israel.

Ps 23:1 - The Lord is my shepherd; I shall not want.

Ps 91:14-16 - Because he hath set his love upon me, therefore will I deliver him: I will set him on high, because he hath known my name. 15 He shall call upon me, and I will answer him: I will be with him in trouble; I will deliver him, and honour him. 16 With long life will I satisfy him, and shew him my salvation.

Ps 103:7 - He made known his ways unto Moses, his acts unto the children of Israel.

Rev 21:1-4 - And I saw a new heaven and a new earth: for the first heaven and the first earth were passed away; and there was no more sea.

Rev 10:9-10 - And I went unto the angel, and said unto him, Give me the little book. And he said unto me, Take it, and eat it up; and it shall make thy belly bitter, but it shall be in thy mouth sweet as honey.

10 And I took the little book out of the angel's hand, and ate it up; and it was in my mouth sweet as honey: and as soon as I had eaten it, my belly was bitter.

Rev 21:1-4 - And I saw a new heaven and a new earth: for the first heaven and the first earth were passed away; and there was no more sea.

2 And I John saw the holy city, new Jerusalem, coming down from God out of heaven, prepared as a bride adorned for her husband.

3 And I heard a great voice out of heaven saying, Behold, the tabernacle of God is with men, and he will dwell with them, and they shall be his people, and God himself shall be with them, and be their God.

4 And God shall wipe away all tears from their eyes; and there shall be no more death, neither sorrow, nor crying, neither shall there be any more pain: for the former things are passed away.

Rom 3:3-4 - For what if some did not believe? shall their unbelief make the faith of God without effect? 4 God forbid: yea, let God be true, but every man a liar; as it is written, That thou mightest be justified in thy sayings, and mightest overcome when thou art judged.

Rom 10:6 - But the righteousness which is of faith speaketh on this wise, …

Rom 11:29 - 29 For the gifts and calling of God are without repentance.

Rom 12:3- For I say, through the grace given unto me, to every man that is among you, not to think of himself more highly than he ought to think; but to think soberly, according as God hath dealt to every man the measure of faith.

Rom 15:1 - We then that are strong ought to bear the infirmities of the weak, and not to please ourselves.

CHAPTER SIX

THE SUPERNATURAL: THE PLACE
I MEET GOD (ELOHIM)

Names of God: https://www.hebrew4christians.com/index.html https://www. hebrew4christians.com/Names_of_G-d/Elohim/elohim.html

1 Thess 5:21- Prove all things; hold fast that which is good.

2 Cor 5:10 - For we must all appear before the judgment seat of Christ; that every one may receive the things done in his body, according to that he hath done, whether it be good or bad.

2 Cor 10:4-6 - (For the weapons of our warfare are not carnal, but mighty through God to the pulling down of strong holds;)

5 Casting down imaginations, and every high thing that exalteth itself against the knowledge of God, and bringing into captivity every thought to the obedience of Christ;

6 And having in a readiness to revenge all disobedience, when your obedience is fulfilled.

Amos 3:7- Surely the Lord God will do nothing, but he revealeth his secret unto his servants the prophets.

Eccl 3:1 - To every thing there is a season, and a time to every purpose under the heaven:

Gal 3:13-14 - Christ hath redeemed us from the curse of the law, being made a curse for us: for it is written, Cursed is every one that hangeth on a tree:

14 That the blessing of Abraham might come on the Gentiles through Jesus Christ; that we might receive the promise of the Spirit through faith.

Heb 4:15-16 - For we have not an high priest which cannot be touched with the feeling of our infirmities; but was in all points tempted like as we are, yet without sin.

16 Let us therefore come boldly unto the throne of grace, that we may obtain mercy, and find grace to help in time of need.

Heb 5:12-14 - For when for the time ye ought to be teachers, ye have need that one teach you again which be the first principles of the oracles of God; and are become such as have need of milk, and not of strong meat.

13 For every one that useth milk is unskilful in the word of righteousness: for he is a babe.

14 But strong meat belongeth to them that are of full age, even those who by reason of use have their senses exercised to discern both good and evil.

Luke 9:1-2 - Then he called his twelve disciples together, and gave them power and authority over all devils, and to cure diseases. 2 And he sent them to preach the kingdom of God, and to heal the sick.

Luke 11:13 - If ye then, being evil, know how to give good gifts unto your children: how much more shall your heavenly Father give the Holy Spirit to them that ask him?

John 1:1-5 - In the beginning was the Word, and the Word was with God, and the Word was God.

2 The same was in the beginning with God.

3 All things were made by him; and without him was not any thing made that was made.

4 In him was life; and the life was the light of men.

5 And the light shineth in darkness; and the darkness comprehended it not.

Mark 16:17-20 - And these signs shall follow them that believe; In my name shall they cast out devils; they shall speak with new tongues;

18 .They shall take up serpents; and if they drink any deadly thing, it shall not hurt them; they shall lay hands on the sick, and they shall recover.

19 So then after the Lord had spoken unto them, he was received up into heaven, and sat on the right hand of God.

20 And they went forth, and preached everywhere, the Lord working with them, and confirming the word with signs following. Amen.

Matt 6:8 - Be not ye therefore like unto them: for your Father knoweth what things ye have need of, before ye ask him.

Matt 10:8 - Heal the sick, cleanse the lepers, and raise the dead, cast out devils: freely ye have received, freely give.

Matt 17:19- Then came the disciples to Jesus apart, and said, Why could not we cast him out?

Matt 18:10 - Take heed that ye despise not one of these little ones; for I say unto you, That in heaven their angels do always behold the face of my Father which is in heaven.

Ps 103:2 - Bless the Lord, O my soul, and forget not all his benefits:

Rom 1:28-32- And even as they did not like to retain God in their knowledge, God gave them over to a reprobate mind, to do those things which are not convenient;

29 Being filled with all unrighteousness, fornication, wickedness, covetousness, maliciousness; full of envy, murder, debate, deceit, malignity; whisperers,

30 Backbiters, haters of God, despiteful, proud, boasters, inventors of evil things, disobedient to parents,

31 Without understanding, covenantbreakers, without natural affection, implacable, unmerciful:

32 Who knowing the judgment of God, that they which commit such things are worthy of death, not only do the same, but have pleasure in them that do them.

Rom 8:26 - Likewise the Spirit also helpeth our infirmities: for we know not what we should pray for as we ought: but the Spirit itself maketh intercession for us with groanings which cannot be uttered.

CHAPTER SEVEN

PROPHECY: THE SUPERNATURAL MOVE OF GOD

Scripture:

1 Cor 13:9-10 For we know in part, and we prophesy in part.

10 But when that which is perfect is come, then that which is in part shall be done away.

1 John 4:1-3 - Beloved, believe not every spirit, but try the spirits whether they are of God: because many false prophets are gone out into the world.

2 Hereby know ye the Spirit of God: Every spirit that confesseth that Jesus Christ is come in the flesh is of God:

1 Sam 15:22 - And Samuel said, Hath the Lord as great delight in burnt offerings and sacrifices, as in obeying the voice of the Lord? Behold, to obey is better than sacrifice, and to hearken than the fat of rams.

1 Sam 16:1 - And the Lord said unto Samuel, How long wilt thou mourn for Saul, seeing I have rejected him from reigning over Israel?

1 Sam 16:6-7 ...fill thine horn with oil, and go, I will send thee to Jesse the Bethlehemite: for I have provided me a king among his sons.

6 And it came to pass, when they were come, that he looked on Eliab, and said, Surely the Lord's anointed is before him.

7 But the Lord said unto Samuel, Look not on his countenance, or on the height of his stature; because I have refused him: for the Lord seeth not as man seeth; for man looketh on the outward appearance, but the Lord looketh on the heart.

2 Tim 2:15 - Study to shew thyself approved unto God, a workman that needeth not to be ashamed, rightly dividing the word of truth.

Amos 3:7 - Surely the Lord God will do nothing, but he revealeth his secret unto his servants the prophets.

Jonah 4:1- But it displeased Jonah exceedingly, and he was very angry.

Eph 4:11-13 - And he gave some, apostles; and some, prophets; and some, evangelists; and some, pastors and teachers;

12 For the perfecting of the saints, for the work of the ministry, for the edifying of the body of Christ: 13 Till we all come in the unity of the faith, and of the knowledge of the Son of God, unto a perfect man, unto the measure of the stature of the fulness of Christ.

CHAPTER EIGHT

BIBLICAL RESTORATION

1 Sam 28:7 - Then said Saul unto his servants, Seek me a woman that hath a familiar spirit, that I may go to her, and inquire of her. And his servants said to him, Behold, there is a woman that hath a familiar spirit at Endor.

1 Sam 30:8 - And David inquired at the Lord, saying, Shall I pursue after this troop? shall I overtake them? And he answered him, Pursue: for thou shalt surely overtake them, and without fail recover all.

1 Sam 30:18-19 - And David recovered all that the Amalekites had carried away: and David rescued his two wives.

19 And there was nothing lacking to them, neither small nor great, neither sons nor daughters, neither spoil, nor any thing that they had taken to them: David recovered all.

1 Thess 5:21- Prove (test) all things; hold fast that which is good.

2 Cor 5:10 - For we must all appear before the judgment seat of Christ; that every one may receive the things done in his body, according to that he hath done, whether it be good or bad.

2 Cor 10:4-6 - (For the weapons of our warfare are not carnal, but mighty through God to the pulling down of strong holds;)

5 Casting down imaginations, and every high thing that exalteth itself against the knowledge of God, and bringing into captivity every thought to the obedience of Christ;

6 And having in a readiness to revenge all disobedience, when your obedience is fulfilled.

2 Cor 11:14- And no marvel; for Satan himself is transformed into an angel of light.

Amos 3:7 - Surely the Lord God will do nothing, but he revealeth his secret unto his servants the prophets.

Eccl 3:1- To everything there is a season, and a time to every purpose under the heaven:

Ex 10:22-23- And Moses stretched forth his hand toward heaven; and there was a thick darkness in all the land of Egypt three days:

23 They saw not one another, neither rose any from his place for three days: but all the children of Israel had light in their dwellings.

Gal 3:13-14 - Christ hath redeemed us from the curse of the law, being made a curse for us: for it is written, Cursed is every one that hangeth on a tree:

14 That the blessing of Abraham might come on the Gentiles through Jesus Christ; that we might receive the promise of the Spirit through faith.

Heb 4:15-16 - For we have not an high priest(Jesus) which cannot be touched with the feeling of our infirmities; but was in all points tempted like as we are, yet without sin.16 Let us therefore come boldly unto the throne of grace, that we may obtain mercy, and find grace to help in time of need.

Heb 8:6 - But now hath he obtained a more excellent ministry, by how much also he is the mediator of a better covenant, which was established upon better promises.

James 1:3-4 - Knowing this, that the trying of your faith worketh patience.

4 But let patience have her perfect work, that ye may be perfect and entire, wanting nothing.

John 1:1-5 - In the beginning was the Word, and the Word was with God, and the Word was God.

2 The same was in the beginning with God.

3 All things were made by him; and without him was not anything made that was made.

4 In him was life; and the life was the light of men.

5 And the light shineth in darkness; and the darkness comprehended it not.

Lev 6:4-5 - Then it shall be, because he hath sinned, and is guilty, that he shall restore that which he took violently away, or the thing which he hath deceitfully gotten, or that which was delivered him to keep, or the lost thing which he found,

5 Or all that about which he hath sworn falsely; he shall even restore it in the principal, and shall add the fifth part more thereto, and give it unto him to whom it appertaineth, in the day of his trespass offering.

Lev 19:31 - Regard not them that have familiar spirits, neither seek after wizards, to be defiled by them: I am the Lord your God.

Luke 11:13 - If ye then, being evil(natural), know how to give good gifts unto your children: how much more shall your heavenly Father give the Holy Spirit (supernatural) to them that ask him?

Mark 6:47-51 - And when even was come, the ship was in the midst of the sea, and he alone on the land. 48 And he saw them toiling in rowing; for the wind was contrary unto them: and about the fourth watch of the night (between 3-6 o'clock) he cometh unto them, walking upon the sea, and <u>would have passed</u>

by them. 49 But when they saw him walking upon the sea, they supposed it had been a spirit, and cried out:50 For they all saw him, and were troubled.

And immediately he talked with them, and saith unto them, Be of good cheer: it is I; be not afraid. 51 And he went up unto them into the ship; and the wind ceased: and they were sore amazed in themselves beyond measure, and wondered.

Matt 5:16 - Let your light so shine before men, that they may see your good works, and glorify your Father which is in heaven.

Matt 6:8 - Be not ye therefore like unto them: for your Father knoweth what things ye have need of, before ye ask him.

Matt 7:11 - If ye then, being evil, know how to give good gifts unto your children, how much more shall your Father which is in heaven give good things to them that ask him?

Matt 18:10- Take heed that ye despise not one of these little ones; for I say unto you, That in heaven their angels do always behold the face of my Father which is in heaven.

Matt 18:16 - But if he will not hear thee, then take with thee one or two more, that in the mouth of two or three witnesses every word may be established.

Matt 22:25-27 - Now there were with us seven brethren: and the first, when he had married a wife, deceased, and, having no issue, left his wife unto his brother:

26 Likewise the second also, and the third, unto the seventh.

27 And last of all the woman died also.

Num 21:9 - And Moses made a serpent of brass, and put it upon a pole, and it came to pass, that if a serpent had bitten any man, when he beheld the serpent of brass, he lived.

Num 22:4-6 - ...And Balak the son of Zippor was king of the Moabites at that time.

5 He sent messengers therefore unto Balaam the son of Beor to Pethor, which is by the river of the land of the children of his people, to call him, saying, Behold, there is a people come out from Egypt: behold, they cover the face of the earth, and they abide over against me:

6 Come now therefore, I pray thee, curse me this people; for they are too mighty for me: peradventure I shall prevail, that we may smite them, and that I may drive them out of the land: for I wot that he whom thou blessest is blessed, and he whom thou cursest is cursed.

Ps 18:29 -For by thee I have run through a troop; and by my God have I leaped over a wall.

Ps 124 - A Song of degrees of David.

1 If it had not been the Lord who was on our side, now may Israel say; 2 If it had not been the Lord who was on our side, when men rose up against us: 3 Then they had swallowed us up quick, when their wrath was kindled against us: 4 Then the waters had overwhelmed us, the stream had gone over our soul:8 Our help is in the name of the Lord, who made heaven and earth.

Rom 1:28-32- And even as they did not like to retain God in their knowledge, God gave them over to a reprobate mind, to do those things which are not convenient;

29 Being filled with all unrighteousness, fornication, wickedness, covetousness, maliciousness; full of envy, murder, debate, deceit, malignity; whisperers,

30 Backbiters, haters of God, despiteful, proud, boasters, inventors of evil things, disobedient to parents,

31 Without understanding, covenant breakers, without natural affection, implacable, unmerciful:

32 Who knowing the judgment of God, that they which commit such things are worthy of death, not only do the same, but have pleasure in them that do them.

Rom 1:28-32- And even as they did not like to retain God in their knowledge, God gave them over to a reprobate mind, to do those things which are not convenient;

29 Being filled with all unrighteousness, fornication, wickedness, covetousness, maliciousness; full of envy, murder, debate, deceit, malignity; whisperers,

30 Backbiters, haters of God, despiteful, proud, boasters, inventors of evil things, disobedient to parents,

31 Without understanding, covenant breakers, without natural affection, implacable, unmerciful:

32 Who knowing the judgment of God, that they which commit such things are worthy of death, not only do the same, but have pleasure in them that do them.

Rom 8:26 - Likewise the Spirit also helpeth our infirmities: for we know not what we should pray for as we ought: but the Spirit itself maketh intercession for us with groanings which cannot be uttered.

Zech 4:6 - Then he answered and spake unto me, saying, This is the word of the Lord unto Zerubbabel, saying, Not by might, nor by power, but by my spirit, saith the Lord of hosts.

CHAPTER NINE

RESTORATION OF THE CHURCH

Acts 2:1-4 - And when the day of Pentecost was fully come, they were all with one accord in one place.

2 And suddenly there came a sound from heaven as of a rushing mighty wind, and it filled all the house where they were sitting. 3 And there appeared unto them cloven tongues like as of fire, and it sat upon each of them. 4 And they were all filled with the Holy Ghost, and began to speak with other tongues, as the Spirit gave them utterance.

Acts 3:20-21 - And he shall send Jesus Christ, which before was preached unto you: 21 Whom the heaven must receive until the times of restitution of all things, which God hath spoken by the mouth of all his holy prophets since the world began.

Gal 4:6 - And because ye are sons, God hath sent forth the Spirit of his Son into your hearts, crying, Abba, Father.

Gen 18:25-26, 32-33 - That be far from thee to do after this manner, to slay the righteous with the wicked: and that the righteous should be as the wicked that be far from thee: Shall not the Judge of all the earth do right? 26 And the Lord said, If I find in Sodom fifty righteous within the city, then I will spare all the place for their sakes. 32 And he said, Oh let not the Lord be angry, and I will speak yet but this once: Peradventure ten shall be found there. And he said,

I will not destroy it for ten's sake. 33 And the Lord went his way, as soon as he had left communing with Abraham: and Abraham returned unto his place.

Hab 2:14 - For the earth shall be filled with the knowledge of the glory of the Lord, as the waters cover the sea.

Isa 1:18-19 - Come now, and let us reason together, saith the Lord: though your sins be as scarlet, they shall be as white as snow; though they be red like crimson, they shall be as wool.

19 If ye be willing and obedient, ye shall eat the good of the land:

Isa 61:3 - To appoint unto them that mourn in Zion, to give unto them beauty for ashes, the oil of joy for mourning, the garment of praise for the spirit of heaviness; that they might be called trees of righteousness, the planting of the Lord, that he might be glorified.

John 14:27 - Peace I leave with you, my peace I give unto you: not as the world giveth, give I unto you. Let not your heart be troubled, neither let it be afraid.

John 16:23-24 - And in that day ye shall ask me nothing. Verily, verily, I say unto you, Whatsoever ye shall ask the Father in my name, he will give it you. 24 Hitherto have ye asked nothing in my name: ask, and ye shall receive, that your joy may be full.

Jonah 1:1-4 - Now the word of the Lord came unto Jonah the son of Amittai, saying,

2 Arise, go to Nineveh, that great city, and cry against it; for their wickedness is come up before me. 3 But Jonah rose up to flee unto Tarshish from the presence of the Lord, and went down to Joppa; and he found a ship going to Tarshish: so he paid the fare thereof, and went down into it, to go with them unto Tarshish from the presence of the Lord. 4 But the Lord sent out a great wind into the sea, and there was a mighty tempest in the sea, so that the ship was like to be broken.

Luke 9:1-2 – Then he called his twelve disciples together, and gave them power and authority over all devils, and to cure diseases.

2 And he sent them to preach the kingdom of God, and to heal the sick.

Luke 10:19 - Behold, I give unto you power to tread on serpents and scorpions, and over all the power of the enemy: and nothing shall by any means hurt you

Luke 23:34 - Then said Jesus, Father, forgive them; for they know not what they do. And they parted his raiment, and cast lots.

Matt 4:4 - But he answered and said, It is written, Man shall not live by bread alone, but by every word that proceedeth out of the mouth of God.

Matt 5:18 - For verily I say unto you, Till heaven and earth pass, one jot or one tittle shall in no wise pass from the law, till all be fulfilled.

Matt 8:5-7 - And when Jesus was entered into Capernaum, there came unto him a centurion, beseeching him, 6 And saying, Lord, my servant lieth at home sick of the palsy, grievously tormented. 7 And Jesus saith unto him, I will come and heal him.

Matt 15:22, 25 - And, behold, a woman of Canaan came out of the same coasts, and cried unto him, saying, Have mercy on me, O Lord, thou Son of David; my daughter is grievously vexed with a devil. 25 Then came she and worshipped him, saying, Lord, help me.

Matt 16:15-19 - He saith unto them, But whom say ye that I am? 16 And Simon Peter answered and said, Thou art the Christ, the Son of the living God. 17 And Jesus answered and said unto him, Blessed art thou, Simon Barjona: for flesh and blood hath not revealed it unto thee, but my Father which is in heaven. 18 And I say also unto thee, That thou art Peter, and upon this rock I will build my church; and the gates of hell shall not prevail against it. 19 And I will give unto thee the keys of the kingdom of heaven: and whatsoever thou shalt bind on earth shall be bound in heaven: and whatsoever thou shalt loose on earth shall be loosed in heaven.

Matt 20:30,32-33 - And, behold, two blind men sitting by the way side, when they heard that Jesus passed by, cried out, saying, Have mercy on us, O Lord, thou Son of David.

32 And Jesus stood still, and called them, and said, What will ye that I shall do unto you?

33 They say unto him, Lord, that our eyes may be opened.

Matt 24:14 - And this gospel of the kingdom shall be preached in all the world for a witness unto all nations; and then shall the end come.

Matt 17:20 - And Jesus said unto them, Because of your unbelief: for verily I say unto you, If ye have faith as a grain of mustard seed, ye shall say unto this mountain, Remove hence to yonder place; and it shall remove; and nothing shall be impossible unto you.

Prov 13:22 - A good man leaveth an inheritance to his children's children: and the wealth of the sinner is laid up for the just.

Ps 103:20 - Bless the Lord, ye his angels, that excel in strength, that do his commandments, hearkening unto the voice of his word.

Rom 8:19-22 - For the earnest expectation of the creature waiteth for the manifestation of the sons of God. 20 For the creature was made subject to vanity, not willingly, but by reason of him who hath subjected the same in hope, 21 Because the creature itself also shall be delivered from the bondage of corruption into the glorious liberty of the children of God. 22 For we know that the whole creation groaneth and travaileth in pain together until now.

CHAPTER TEN

DAUGHTERS OF ZION

Ps 100:1-5 - Make a joyful noise unto the Lord, all ye lands.

2 Serve the Lord with gladness: come before his presence with singing.

3 Know ye that the Lord he is God: it is he that hath made us, and not we ourselves; we are his people, and the sheep of his pasture.

4 Enter into his gates with thanksgiving, and into his courts with praise: be thankful unto him, and bless his name.

5 For the Lord is good; his mercy is everlasting; and his truth endureth to all generations.

Heb 1:1-4 - God, who at sundry times and in divers manners spake in time past unto the fathers by the prophets,

2 Hath in these last days spoken unto us by his Son, whom he hath appointed heir of all things, by whom also he made the worlds;

3 Who being the brightness of his glory, and the express image of his person, and upholding all things by the word of his power, when he had by himself purged our sins, sat down on the right hand of the Majesty on high;

4 Being made so much better than the angels, as he hath by inheritance obtained a more excellent name than they.

THE AUTHOR

PROPHETESS RENA WILBURN

Daughters of Zion Ministries

"Blessings"

A chosen vessel, gifted, and a giver of "self" are genuine words describing Prophetess Rena Wilburn. Expounding the word of God powerfully shows her dedication, discipline, and diligence. "Unifying the Body of Christ" a higher calling, influences, motivates, and challenges her to reach for excellence.

Leaving her Computer Consulting position, travel now allows Prophetess Wilburn opportunities to minister a prophetic, preaching, teaching, and healing ministry to an audience of excited believers, proclaiming the gospel of Jesus Christ on radio, television, and prayer lines, thus fulfills the Great Commission and the personal mandate: "We Speak To Nations - With One Voice." She awaits publishing her new book: "The SuperNatural: The Place I Meet God."

Prophetess Wilburn is the mother of a dynamic and recent college graduate (Kristin Wilburn) who shares the same prophetic anointing with a desire to open her own Youth Center. One of Prophetess Wilburn's greatest passions is to see the Body of Christ walking in the gifting for which God has called by the aid of the Holy Spirit.

Daughters of Zion host Women Seminars design to unite, educate and minister to the needs of women. Training, Accountability, and the necessity of covering are crucial in the Body of Christ; therefore, she has several ministry overseers and affiliations.

Prophetess Wilburn believes that "One word from God can change anything." Having studied with some of the great teachers of this age and the constant study of the Bible has given her the knowledge base to minister to God's people effectively. Her hardest but the most rewarding class was "The Art of Hearing God" by John Paul Jackson. Prophetess stated, "It will test all that is both theoretical and practical in the gifting of prophetic anointing. Prepare for Change!

Printed in the United States
by Baker & Taylor Publisher Services